*Brave New Voices*

# Brave New Voices

## The Youth Speaks Guide to Teaching Spoken-Word Poetry

JEN WEISS
SCOTT HERNDON

Foreword by Tracie Morris

HEINEMANN
Portsmouth, NH

Heinemann

361 Hanover Street
Portsmouth, NH 03801–3912
www.heinemann.com

*Offices and agents throughout the world*

Please visit the Youth Speaks website at: www.youthspeaks.org.

The authors and publisher wish to thank those who have generously given permission to reprint borrowed material:

Excerpt from the article "2nd Suspect Held in Slay of Teen" by Richard Weir is reprinted from *The Daily News*, January 17, 2001. Copyright © 2001 by New York Daily News, L. P. Reprinted with permission.

Excerpt from "Gangsta Suite" by Tracie Morris is reprinted by permission of Soft Skull Press.

Excerpt from *Revolutionary Voices* by Tim Arevalo is reprinted by permission of the author. Published by Alyson Books, 2000.

**Library of Congress Cataloging-in-Publication Data**
Weiss, Jen.
    Brave new voices : the Youth Speaks guide to teaching spoken-word poetry / Jen Weiss, Scott Herndon.
        p. cm.
    Includes bibliographical references.
    ISBN 0-86709-508-3 (acid-free paper)
    1. Poetry—Authorship—Study and teaching. 2. Oral interpretation of poetry—Study and teaching. 3. Creative writing—Study and teaching.   I. Herndon, Scott, 1972–
II. Youth Speaks (Organization).   III. Title.

PE1404 .W452 2001
808.1'071'2–dc21                                        2001039160

*Editor:* William Varner
*Production editor:* Sonja S. Chapman
*Cover design:* Josh Worth
*Manufacturing:* Steve Bernier

Printed in the United States of America on acid-free paper
T & C Digital

*For Robert Herndon*
*August 28, 1943–February 23, 2000*
*and*
*Marcella Kirby Ryan Morris*
*March 25, 1921–February 3, 1998*

# Contents

# Foreword

What's a good poem? These days, the polarity between the two general answers to this question has rarely been as divergent. This book seeks a sort of hand holding between academically driven and performance poetry schools. What this text-based introductory course provides is an opportunity to honor the intent of poetry——to move people in head and heart——without wasting words.

This is a guide to *creating* poetry on the page and in live presentations. While enjoyable in process and result, the suggestions are also empowering, by helping people think and feel deeply in the company of others. The engagement of the artist (and the artist-to-be) in the process of discovering themselves as part of a community (where artists and non-artists intersect) is crucial. It opens up the artist to collective memory and creation. It provides an antidote to the isolating, "art star" and/or elitist academic environments that "validate" artists.

These exclusionary viewpoints underscore artistic "legitimacy" but increase a sense of artistic dis-empowerment. What the Youth Speaks program presents is a more holistic, and dare I say, *realistic* vantage from which to cultivate the art of poetry. We are part of intersecting communities. We relate to each other as beings on the planet, caring humans, members of socially-designated roles, and as creative entities. To a great degree it is the isolated, ivory-tower artist and solitary performer persona that are the mythology. For no one can live, much less make art, alone.

*Brave New Voices* reinforces this idea/ideal of community in form and content. In form, for example, the book presents accessible chapters that pair emerging and established artists in opening quotes. This underscores the concept of the harmony in this community while presenting the importance and priority of young people in making this work go forward. The egalitarianism among the students is also key. There is an extraordinary attention here to the students who have something powerful to say but who aren't "in the limelight." It is a breakthrough of the stratification that can cripple the creativity of young people at this crux in their lives. Inter-generational, the opening chapter quotes emphasize the transformations of the students and the teacher.

In content the focus on process, kindness, and strong writing skills helps build poetic "musculature" which instills confidence humanely. In an overall sense, this guide elucidates the potential for all of us to grow, change, and improve our personal and our community's environment.

Another important component is how Jen and Scott's book presents not only individual development but explores poetic *movements* in context. By complementing the current Hip Hop inspired momentum of today's poetry with that of the Beats we see several aspects of a similar continuum. Not only because the Beat Movement was also inspired by African-American culture (generally through Jazz music and specifically through African-American poets such as Baraka/Jones, Kaufman, and Joans) but like Hip Hop, both movements emerged from rigor, enjoyment, and uncompromising community engagement, as well as a critique of the regressive artistic and political "status quo."

On a personal level, I've experienced the Youth Speaks dynamic directly, as a workshop leader and observer. I was energized by its collective spirit, which was motivational, and simultaneously and importantly, de-emphasized competitiveness. I was greatly honored when this organization created an award in my name. Their attention to developing poetry for two-dimensional (page) and three-dimensional (stage) environments without forcing the students to choose between them is what I strive for as an artist and teacher. The aesthetics infused in the Youth Speaks program is a more advanced point of view than those in some ivyed institutes of higher education. Affirming the cultural contexts of the individual and the groups they come from adds another fundamental form of harmony to this process.

The five-week program is exciting! As a teacher, don't be surprised if in this process, your students surpass their expectations—and yours. Be prepared to expand your own level of consciousness and assumptions about what poets, and particularly young poets, should be saying. It may even be healthy for you to try these exercises yourself. However, I would caution you to not do them *with* your students in class (you should give students space to explore without forcing them, deliberately or inadvertently, to compare themselves with your work or expectations). You will find an astounding new level of intimacy and trust in your relationship with your students. What you may find is that they respect you more and in a more loving way. What you may have to give up is your sense of privilege, hierarchy, and domination over them. But it is from that unconditional trust that students learn the lessons in your classroom and for their lives. And, selfishly, it is through their growth that we, as educators, find fulfillment.

So, the question I'd pose as an educator after working with this program is, why limit these techniques to high school-age youth? This guide provides a forum for all of us: students, teachers, parents, workshop leaders, and friends to bring this loving, demanding, and spirit-enhancing work into all our lives. We can be free to be students ourselves and allow them to teach us. I would expand the applicability of this content to a range of ages, demographics, cultures, and sub-cultures. Imagine giving the elderly permission to express themselves artistically on multiple levels, without judgment. Or Bi-lingual/multi-lingual people who feel ashamed for the many words they have at their disposal, only some of which, are in English. How about any person who is cut off from their feelings for various reasons? Again, young people in our society give us the opportunity to show how promising the future can be. As they develop themselves and develop in this process they make it possible to expand our own horizons as adults. What's a good poem?: A poem that doesn't make you have to choose how to feel it. When the writer works at being better for having written it and we feel differently having experienced it.

I wish all the students and educators in formal and informal capacities, great luck, success, and new knowledge in their multiple layers of being. And I thank them for inspiring Jen and Scott who so thoughtfully bring this wisdom to all of us.

—Tracie Morris

# Acknowledgments

Where would we be without our teachers, our friends, our students, our families?

To our teachers: A heartfelt thank you to Teachers and Writers Collaborative, especially Nancy Larson Shapiro, whose generosity gave Youth Speaks a home in New York, whose dedication to poetry meant supporting our loud and bustling workshops day after day, and whose comments were seminal to the creation of these pages. And thank you Pat Hoy, Alfred Guy, and Darlene Forrest at New York University and Peter Finley at Cal State-Stanislaus for your help when this book was at best a tangled conversation. Thank you to Bill Varner at Heinemann for your unremitting support of our project.

To our friends and colleagues: Thank you to James Kass for your vision, and to Dave Yanofsky for your dedication. Thank you to the mentors of Youth Speaks for doing what you do and believing in it. Special thanks to Robyn Rodgers, Tim Arevalo, Rachel Posner, Bob Holman, Maureen Weiss, Celena Glenn, and Abiodun Oyewole for your help and your wisdom. Thank you to the spoken-word poetry community at large for being there to assist, to perform, to teach, and to write.

To our students: Thank you all for your voices, for your profoundly poetic sensibilities, for your ceaseless energy as we play in the interstices between ideas and words, and for your brilliant and courageous performances on and off the stage.

Last, to our families: What words of thanks can we offer those who instilled in us the desire to write and teach? So much needs to be written, and perhaps the best place to start is with you, as we discover the magnitude of the gift you continue to give us.

# Introduction

*Youth Speaks has helped me understand that I am capable of saying something powerful. This fall alone I learned about the importance of collaborating with my peers, of finding other young people who are active, aware, fed up, confused, scared, but motivated . . . above all, motivated. These workshops have helped me keep focused on my writing by learning to accept the criticism of people I respect and people whose lives, however different from each other, come together with a desire to do more, to bring our creativity to a higher level, to understand with hopes of also being understood.*

—Vanessa Tobar, 17

*What I am describing here is a mode of utopian thinking: thinking that refuses mere compliance, that looks down roads not yet taken to the shapes of a more fulfilling social order, to more vibrant ways of being in the world. This kind of reshaping imagination may be released through many sorts of dialogue: dialogue among the young who come from different cultures and different modes of life.*

—Maxine Greene (1995, 5)

## A Personal Story

In the few short years I have been directing Youth Speaks in New York, I have seen every type of teenager develop into a poet. From Brooklyn to Queens, from housing projects to the Upper East Side, out of public and private schools, these poets are coming forward and speaking up. Backpacks loaded with composition books and ballpoint pens, they swap rhymes and heroic couplets after school, memorize their poems on subways and street corners, perform in venues around town. And this is happening on a national scale, in New York and the San Francisco Bay area; in Ann Arbor, Michigan, and Taos, New Mexico.

I came to teen spoken-word poetry as an admirer of it. When I was living in San Francisco, I discovered Youth Speaks through the annual Teen Poetry Slam. It was amazing! Never had I been around such diverse groups of people nor known such an exciting community of poets. Youth Speaks is about youth, but the people involved in it are adults, vibrant and poetic, mostly teachers of one thing or another. In 1999, I piloted the program in New York City through Teachers and Writers Collaborative. I ultimately started teaching, and then, with the help of other mentors, shaped our workshops for teenagers into thirteen-week creative writing and spoken-word workshops. Today the program thrives, and I'm thrilled to be around young writers as often as I am. Watching them confront their issues in writing reminds me of my own discovery of poetry when I was in high school, how it fed me even when what I needed to say remained elusive and difficult to express.

I have worked with hundreds of teenagers in high school, but mostly as part of Youth Speaks' after-school program. The gift of it comes every time I hear a teenager say what they mean clearly and with confidence. After they've spent some time in the program, I send teenagers into high school classrooms to pitch poetry to other teenagers. Commanding the rapt attention of their peers, diverse teens turn out in droves for our annual Teen Poetry Slam, spoken-word workshops, and ongoing open mic series.

The more teenagers I meet, the more I realize how many are writing, often in isolation, without even the sense that what they are writing is important. Many of these youths are natural per-formers, rhythmically moving in and out of language (*freestyling*); others are quiet observers of the world around them. They come in every form—rappers, street poets, closet artists. They stay in the program because they have discovered a community in one another, something they urgently need. As one student said about discovering Youth Speaks,

> It was destiny. At first, I felt like a rebel because I thought that I had a harder life story than the other teens. But what I found out was that we all had similar

experiences. I realized that I could begin to accept other people for who they were despite our differences in background. I figured if these people could hear me, then those from my background could hear me too. The response to my poetry was like a dream.

I feel invigorated when I am around teenagers these days. I know poetry is alive.

—*Jen Weiss*

Like you, we love the students we teach. For all of us involved in Youth Speaks, the best teachers teach out of their own passion. Ours is spoken-word poetry. In sharing our teaching methods with you, we hope that our ideas will enrich not only other after-school writing programs, but also high school English classes across the country. Even if we can't start up after-school programs everywhere, we want to put poetry into the hands of as many teenagers as we can. Our strongest connection is through you, our community of dedicated and passionate teachers.

## Youth Speaks Pedagogy and the History of Spoken Word

### PEDAGOGY

There is a direct connection between teenagers' written and vocal worlds. By combining the two through spoken-word poetry, we encourage young people not only to think, but also to find the clearest path possible by which to communicate. We begin with this: Whatever teenagers are saying, we want to hear it. Within a peer-workshop setting, we want to give our students the tools to justify, expand, and enrich their own processes as thinkers and writers. After all, there are many poets in a classroom who feel alienated when it comes to writing their thoughts down on paper, but who can mesmerize their peers with spoken verbal flows. We want to reward both academically gifted writers and alienated performers—writers who express themselves in rap, visual art, and performance. By bringing these performers and writers together and encouraging the development of both, we support more than one kind of student. Whether they are mixing metaphors, exchanging meter for rhyme, or letting lyric forefront line break, teenagers are using poetry first and foremost to tell their stories. Wherever their creative journeys take them, though they often better their craft, teenagers need to define "good poetry" for themselves. Our job is to guide and support our students along the way.

If we are to teach our students poetry of any kind, we must acknowledge what they bring to the table. Youth Speaks promotes an environment open to questions of identity, race, gender, sexuality, socioeconomic issues, and politics. Rather than treat teenagers' problems as though they don't exist, we want to embrace the complicated web of obstacles and achievements teenagers encounter as fertile ground for setting the writing process in motion. If a young writer questions herself and feels supported along the way, then gets to the level of performing her poetry for her peers, she comes closer to understanding herself in the context of others. We strive to provide a community that recognizes and works to address the concerns of what Jabari Mahiri (1998) describes as

> students struggl[ing] with complex issues of representation as they seek out and try on different identities in their passage from youth to adulthood. Yet the systematic absence of representation or the calculated misrepresentation of youth as well as people of color often stifles their attempts to define and understand both their distinctiveness and their similarities. (55)

The first step is to make the teenagers we work with feel like they belong to each other. In this respect, the importance of our emphasis on performance cannot be overstated. At first, performances offer us access to what our students are writing and an opportunity to hear each others' voices. As our students begin to know and trust each other, our next step is to make them feel like they belong to the world of writing. And there is no more accessible portal to that world than spoken-word poetry.

## A Brief History of Spoken Word

Spoken-word poetry consists of an interplay of various art forms. It is a modern-day poetic form rooted in the oral traditions of African griots, the blues, Baptist preaching, and storytelling. In recent decades, we find strains of it in the free-association methods of the surrealists and in the protest songs and poems of the antiwar, feminist, and civil rights movements. We heard it in the fifties, sixties, and seventies from the Beats, Gil Scot-Heron, and the Last Poets, among others. The center of the recent bloom of spoken word is the Nuyorican Poets Café and Bar 13 in New York City. The café, a hotbed since the mid-eighties, continues to host a packed Friday-night slam and is a regular venue for Youth Speaks' annual slams and open mic events.

Spoken word today draws upon these historical influences as much as it does upon hip-hop and other music, pop culture, vernacular speech, and traditional poetry. It is a performance-oriented poetry the best examples of which begin with a precise and well-*written* poem.

It is essential to recognize spoken word as a multilayered art form, especially when engaging teenagers. Their natural alacrity for spoken word is no doubt linked to the prevalent influence of hip-hop culture, which is itself multifaceted. Ask a teenager who her favorite poet is and you're likely to hear a range of answers: Ani DiFranco, Tupac Shakur, Sylvia Plath, Mos Def, Edgar Allan Poe, Maya Angelou, Saul Williams.

As a mode of expression for and by teenagers, spoken word sprang onto the San Francisco scene through Youth Speaks, which was founded in 1997 by James Kass. In its grassroots stages, Youth Speaks sought to give young writers an outlet for performing poetry. Today it is a thriving bicoastal, not-for-profit organization dedicated to the free and undaunted expression of teenagers. Youth Speaks offers San Francisco and New York City teenagers free writing and spoken-word resources. For six years, adult writers like us have been mentoring teenagers interested in writing and performing their poetry. By drawing upon the rich culture of the slam community to emphasize performing poetry as well as writing it, we seduced a whole new audience of teenagers into turning the powerful gears of poetry.

We receive many requests from teachers, parents, teenagers, and writers across the country who are interested in setting up a program like Youth Speaks. The recipe is simple: We combine an after-school writing workshop program, an ongoing noncompetitive youth open mic series, an annual teen poetry slam, an in-school poetry program, and myriad publishing opportunities for exposing teen voices. We recruit teenagers in high schools and at our public performance events. Once we have a handful of articulate, stage-savvy young poets, we offer stipends for them to work in high schools to spread the word about what resources we offer. After all, if something is working for one teenager, many more will follow.

This guide to teaching spoken-word poetry is our effort to share the successes of the Youth Speaks program with you. If you are just getting started and don't have poets on hand, videos can be used to get teenagers excited about spoken-word poetry. In 1999, Straight Ahead Productions completed a feature-length documentary on the youth spoken-word movement, *Poetic License*. Among other things, this film celebrates dedicated programs like Youth Speaks. It is a detailed account of the National Teen Poetry Slam in Albuquerque, New Mexico, and features many poets who found spoken-word poetry through our program. The educational version of this film was made specifically with teachers in mind and is available as a supplement to this guide.

## An Overview of This Book

Teaching spoken-word poetry to teenagers is fairly straightforward when you couple exposure to different types of writing with an environment that's conducive to free expression. In the following chapters, you will uncover a terrain to explore. We suggest you modify our themes and exercises to fit your students' interests. If teaching spoken-word poetry is new to you, you will experience certain roadblocks, as we sometimes do. We try to think of these roadblocks as evidence that the project matters, rather than as a reason to be afraid. Above all, we take into account our students' backgrounds, areas of influence, and artistic familiarity— and if we perceive these things as roadblocks, we shift our emphasis away from what we wish our students knew or had read in order to listen to what they are saying. Our teaching succeeds when it helps improve what our students are saying.

We are convinced that the workshops described in this book will reward teachers as much as they will enhance teen writers' educations. This book came directly out of our own teaching. In the time we have been teaching spoken-word poetry, we have learned immensely from those involved in the Youth Speaks program. Much of the material in the following chapters comes directly out of the complex interchange between our mentors and our students, and from our commitment to learning from the teenagers themselves. Their feedback and poetry have informed our work every step of the way.

This book maps a workshop course that can be given one, two, or three days a week for roughly five weeks. Though most of our teaching takes place in an after-school workshop setting, we have modified our curriculum to work in a high school English classroom. The workshop culminates in a public event, either a poetry slam or an open mic. We have provided a brief glossary at the end of this guide. As much as possible, we have minimized the use of the kinds of poetic terms and explications that usually fill poetry guidebooks, because what is needed is not an archival knowledge of the mechanics of poetry, but an open mind, an enthusiastic demeanor, and the ability to draw students into listening to one another more attentively and to writing *more*.

The book is a guide for teachers who want to be involved in the creative lives of their students. In the broadest sense, that means participating in developing students' writing, thinking, and performance skills. Because spoken-word poetry draws upon music and pop culture as much as it grows out of reading the poetic canon, this book is also for teachers who want to learn from the complicated interactions between teenagers and the manifold layers of their culture—hip-hop lyrics, teen politics, issues of love and loss, and so on.

The chapters demonstrate how spoken-word poetry can be used as a tool for interweaving creative expression, writing, and performance. Each chapter discusses one week of the workshop in terms of both pedagogical method and content themed by a topic relevant to the week in which it occurs, in a trajectory hoping to culminate in a public poetry event. The chapters generally move from pedagogical method and the content of the week, to the workshop's poetic concerns inherent in them, to practical exercises and helpful hints. By content we mean both poetic technique and the tradition which helps to elucidate it. And because our teaching benefits most from exchanges between teachers and students, each chapter ends with a student profile and interview pertaining to the subject at hand, and we used poems by those students to illustrate devices and techniques and the outcome of a featured exercise.

Each chapter of this book elaborates on the definition of spoken-word poetry and its relationship to traditional poetic forms. Chapter 1 begins by mapping the pedagogical space that teachers must establish in order to get a diverse workshop started, while the later chapters provide concrete and practical workshop tools.

We have only begun to tap into this reservoir for teaching poetry to teenagers, so this book doesn't answer all the questions there are about spoken-word poetry. As you begin exploring spoken-word poetry, consider the ebb and flow of your students' voices as you read these chapters. The ideas you develop will help shape this rich resource.

# week 1 ■ Getting Started

*I can't even believe how much better my work is after*
*taking this workshop. Not only did I learn some really*
*great techniques and classic writing styles and forms, but my*
*writing is so much freer now. It just has this more authentic*
*free flow style to it. I learned how to just spill my thoughts*
*onto the page without any restraint or precaution.*

—Kazmira Pitlak, 17

*Poetry is the way we help give name to the nameless*
*so it can be thought. The farthest horizons of our hopes*
*and fears are cobbled by our poems, carved from the*
*rock experiences of our daily lives.*

—Audre Lorde (1996, 37)

## Parameters: Preparing for the Workshop

As teachers preparing to conduct a five-week workshop on
spoken-word poetry, our first aim is to create a setting that
allows for the widest possible acceptance of student voices and
concerns. To do so, we may need to step out of our standard
roles as teachers and into roles that we and our students
actively define. This may mean treating everyone in the class,
including ourselves, on a first-name basis, or calling ourselves
mentors instead of teachers. We should trust—as we do in performing most difficult tasks—that the simplest, most direct
changes can lead to positive results down the road.

1

What other concrete suggestions can help us get the workshop started? Here is a simple checklist of practical and helpful parameters for a productive workshop. If you need more guidelines than these, we encourage you to design your own.

1. *Reinvigorate the traditional classroom space.* Structuring the classroom space around the students tells them that the workshop is for *them*. Similarly, switching the seating order every day reintroduces long-familiar students to each other as poets. Given that high school classrooms are often spaces of peer judgment and grades long before they become arenas for honest and free-flowing expression, you must recreate your space at the outset of the workshop. It will take a little imagination from everyone involved, but it can and should be done.

2. *Let the workshop be student-driven.* To facilitate the greatest possible communication between student and workshop, make as many ideas for discussion as possible emerge from and revolve around your students' work. First, try to avoid teaching only the topics you're interested in. Second, dedicate at least half of each class to the performance of student work. Cutting back on how much you speak is often the first step in making the workshop act for itself. These two strategies ensure that the writing your students offer will reflect the most important, urgent, and suggestive topics—for you as well as them. (There are ways to spur your students to write poems that touch upon the things *you'd* like to discuss while giving the essential impression that the topics originated from the students themselves. We list a few of these strategies later in this chapter.)

3. *Get rid of censorship.* Make the class members feel as free as possible to express themselves. As a mentor, stay focused on your ultimate goals for the workshop, rather than acting with too much vigilance over the use of an offensive word. Allow the students themselves to become the most important critics in the classroom. This will take time and careful tending. Begin by continually asking questions of the entire workshop, following up

on controversial topics by asking the group to think aloud. Knowing when—to disappear on the sidelines, to make a single comment, to thoroughly discuss a hot topic suggested by a student piece—that is what will make us great mentors.

*4. Don't use grades.* It is essential to reward students for their writing, but it's even more important that grades not be used as the primary means of praise. There are no right or wrong answers here, only more and less interesting methods of self-expression. More than anything else, remember that teens need your attention and open-mindedness. For students who shirk writing when it is not graded by the teacher, the fun and challenge of the workshop must provide motivation. Working without grades sounds like a hard job—and it is—but it is difficult because it is important. Very few great poems, if any, were written for a grade.

*5. Find the good in students' work and challenge them to make it better.* In the first few weeks of the workshop, use your authority to earn students' trust. Repeatedly ask the class to focus on the positive aspects of a poem, rather than on what bothers them, and teach them to treat those aspects as the most important ones for improvement. Craft exercises that draw writers into entrusting each other with the crucial job of improving each other's work by the most positive means possible.

*6. Make sure that all exercises are read aloud by every student.* Remember, spoken-word poetry is a poetry of performance. The more students read aloud early in the workshop, the easier it will be for them to make the transition from writing to performing before the entire school. If a student absolutely will not read an exercise, allow for a rare exception—but as soon as the next exercise comes up, all members of the workshop should encourage this student to read.

*7. Experiment.* Good teaching and writing always begin as experiments. Who would perform an experiment in which they understood everything about what was being done, in which there was no risk or uncertainty? Scientists experiment every day in areas that are not understood, thinking hard about solutions and making inroads into areas that previously seemed blocked. So should our student writers, and so should we as teachers.

**8. *Remember that great writing is a process, not a product.*** Think of the coming five weeks as the beginning of a lifetime of writing, rather than as a sort of bootcamp designed to create a few brilliant poems. Instead of being a class in the usual sense of the word, beginning with lessons and ending with a test, the workshop strives to offer the processes and practice necessary for effective writing and performance to take place.

**9. *Have some fun!*** As a mentor gearing up for the first class, be willing to be excited and even afraid; be ready to be alert, engaged and receptive. Promise that you won't expect the world in the first weeks of the workshop, and that you will trust that the poems will develop as the workshop community develops— often when you least expect it. Above all, enter the classroom with exercises and an open mind, then buckle down and do what you do best: teach.

Throughout this chapter, we offer hints that have been helpful for teachers at Youth Speaks. These are not hard-and-fast rules, but reminders to help you navigate through the challenging first week of a performance poetry workshop.


## *The First Day*

We could begin this book with success stories, anecdotes of Youth Speaks teachers who had perfect classes from the beginning. But nothing would be further from the point of this book. All great classes begin with a touch of resistance, and with students demonstrating fear, pride, and vulnerability before deciding to open their hearts and minds to the class. Great teachers know how to work with the initial venting of these emotions and turn them into the class's strength, week by week. We therefore begin this book with the issue of resistance and the discomfort that naturally arises from unfamiliarity. Though these topics are often sources of pain for teachers, they can be addressed in a way that promotes growth from the very beginning of the workshop.

Learning about the sources of a workshop's resistance (and the means for solving it) entails learning about the students and coming to understand the way they interact with their teachers and their peers. As the workshop develops, a growing knowledge of each of the writers in the class will help you design exercises and discussions especially suited to their needs.

When many Youth Speaks teachers first start teaching in the program, their troubles stem from two facts that can take some time to fix: They are terrified of their students, and they are encumbered by high, unrealistic expectations. These are common and forgivable troubles that all teachers deal with at one time or other. We suggest that, rather than giving in to sheer panic, teachers allot a productive place for fear and expectation. Feeling fear tells us that we care about what we are doing in the classroom, that we have a stake and investment in what we are teaching. Rather than a warning sign, then, fear is a good omen for us as teachers. High expectations are often as much tied to the hope that our students will succeed as they are to our desire to personally succeed in the classroom (or to have our students thank us profusely for the gift of our teaching!). These natural feelings, if left unattended, can create a stultifying paradox in the classroom: We will simultaneously expect too little and too much from our students. In the first sense, we protect ourselves by insisting on our own expertise. In the second, we try to bring our students to our own level of expertise without taking the steps necessary to make their journey possible.

On the first day of the workshop, we should recognize that student resistance is almost always not a resistance to *us*, but to the complex web of vulnerabilities they feel in this new and demanding environment. It's important to make a distinction between this *vulnerable resistance* and what we might call *obstinate resistance*. While vulnerable resistance can paralyze an otherwise willing and enthusiastic student, obstinate resistance has more to do with a student's conscious desire to resist the structure of the class, school in general, or even our personalities as teachers. We do everything we can as teachers to organize our five-week workshop around vulnerable resistance—in other words, to believe that we are only one class, one exercise, or one comment away from drawing every one of our enthusiastic writers out of her shell. What does this mean? Practically speaking, it means doing our best to convince ourselves that none of the resistance to the workshop is coming from the obstinate side. This makes sense at an intellectual level as well, because no one knows when even the most obstinate writer will let down her guard and start writing. More often than not, it happens—and when it does, the feeling is electric, because we have earned it.

We cannot simply assert that we will help our students make their poetry beautiful, unless we want to scare them into thinking that the workshop will be about our goals as teachers and not their goals as writers. Our initial goal, then, should *not* be to teach incredible poetry. Instead, it should be a humble one: to bring students to the point at which they begin to show their poetry to the workshop.

In order to make our students' vulnerability productive, we must achieve two things: leveling the playing field and crafting exercises that leave few writers feeling exposed. Students should feel comfortable whether they are strong or weak readers, experienced or new to creative writing, outgoing or introverted. We can achieve this through careful planning, a sensitivity to students' needs, and a little imagination. Until we achieve this crucial step, no workshop will leave the ground—but after we have achieved it, our workshop will be able to surmount almost anything.

Achieving comfort in a classroom is a difficult task that represents a radical departure from the regimented English classes we suffered through when in high school. That experience was something like being in a maximally low security prison where the prisoners sat in rigid rows and memorized rules number one—that there was a canon of poetry to be read (and its parents were Shakespeare, Dickinson, and Frost)—and two—if there were poems to be written, they might as well sound like the poems of the parents, or stumble under the tag of prose.

It was easy to change these rules when we started Youth Speaks—our teens were writing poems in spite of the rules, and everywhere we turned, teachers were asking us what to do with the writing of this next generation.

Thus, on the first day of the workshop, we walk into the class and move the chairs into a semicircle. This is not a new strategy for structuring a creative atmosphere, but it is common because it works, especially if you place students with peers they are not accustomed to having as neighbors. Why? It boils down to a second paradox: While unfamiliarity may be the greatest source of resistance and hand-wringing in your classroom, it is also the most fertile ground for writing poetry. Making the environment new can divert student resistance away from us as teachers toward a less dictatorial impression of power, if only because the traditional arbiter of judgment—the teacher at the head of the class—has suddenly been replaced by students looking to each other for guidance.

It is much more challenging for a mentor to face a workshop of students who know each other already than to face students who are unfamiliar with each other. When the students know each other, you must do extra work to upend the usual relationships between teacher, student, and peer. For the purposes of this chapter, we assume that we are teaching a group of students who know each other.

The object is to lessen the students' sense of familiarity in the classroom, so further reorienting the space is the top priority. We can do this in many ways, from rearranging the chairs, to sitting in the back of the room and beginning the class from there, to playing jazz or bringing in a painting. The mystery of the new placement, location, sound, or object should remain unexplained, so we will teach for as long as possible before explaining why the artwork is leaning against the chalkboard or what the music on the stereo is. The more unfamiliar our students feel in the quite familiar structure of a high school classroom, the better chance we have to break the ice and have some fun.

## Tackling the Personal Challenge: First Exercises

How can we teach the many personalities in our classes without understanding what our own personalities bring to the classroom? The first week of any poetry workshop is invariably awkward. The key to teaching teens creative writing well lies not only in recognizing how we come across, but also in facing the vulnerable resistance that we feel toward our students as we try to create a free and open space for them. Are the students as afraid of us as we are of them? What kind of feedback will we need from our students before we feel comfortable with them?

If we ourselves can confront these questions realistically, we should be able to play the cat-and-mouse game of student questions and teacher responses in the early days of the workshop when we are unfamiliar with each other. The more comfortable we teachers are with our teen writers, the sooner we can begin rewarding them for their attempts to respond to us, setting in motion a cycle of creative expression and critical feedback.

Youth Speaks tackles these challenges head-on by asking our teachers to come into the classroom *expecting* to feel resistant to their students, perhaps even afraid of them at some basic, vulnerable level. This feeling is perfectly natural and it can give us a good sense of what our students are feeling about their own sudden presence in a writing classroom and why they may be behaving as they are. Ultimately, the only way to work through resistance is to get to know our students and to be open to them, not simply in our role as teachers, but as people and mentors who can help unlock the door to a rich life of thinking and poetry.

We do our best to expect nothing on the first day of a workshop save that the members will have some fun, write and perform a good deal of poetry, and get to know each other in the process. This openness is often visible on the teacher's face and in her disposition, and it often has an appreciable effect on the students' initial reception of the workshop. During the first few classes, make it our goal to sense not only how the students are reacting to us, but also how they are reacting to each other and to the work being generated. We craft our later exercises to take advantage of their moods and reactions, choosing the path of least resistance and going with the flow.

Let's say it's the first day of class and all the introductions have been finished. We choose a straightforward writing exercise to begin the workshop—for instance, we ask the students to describe their favorite room, or a room in which two people had a fight. If a student says something silly before we finish describing the assignment, if we hear giggles and get the distinct feeling that the class needs to release some of its energy, fast, we know that this is the time to laugh and let go. Teenagers possess some of the most personally directed wit there is. If we feel like our students want to laugh at everything on the first day, we may change gears by asking them to write a piece in which they make as much fun of an adult as they can. The adult can be the teacher, the principal, an old teacher, or another adult, as long as everyone in the room knows the person. We may even tell the students to give the poem as much bite as possible. The only rules are that the person cannot be a student in the class, and that the person's name remains hidden until the writing is read aloud. When the students perform their pieces, the class tries to decide who the unlucky butt of the joke is. This exercise almost always draws out even the most resistant students and bonds them with the rest of the workshop members, for there is now an inside joke for all involved—including you. Remember: If you face a resistant group, do not lose your confidence or composure. In any group of teenagers, you will find allies in every corner who will con-

tinue to embark on the poetry journey with you. We must trust
that every teenager will experience at least one definite moment
when something they've written is felt by the group as a whole,
and that as a result, a poetic triumph will be recorded forever,
deep in her soul.

What does an exercise like this one achieve? So many
things. For one, it draws the workshop members together in a
collective bond, and for once the teacher is within the secret circle too. This kind of special bond removes the workshop from the
students' other classes, from authority and judgment. It makes
the workshop a creative entity unto itself. Second, an exercise
like this can prepare you to relate to the various insecurities ado-
lescent writers face. Providing an outlet for real feelings can be
the first stone on the path toward teens being able to write honestly about their deepest concerns later in the workshop, when
their writing will really count. One thing is certain from the first
day on: Teens will never write honestly if they sense that teachers cannot or will not try to relate to them, or if they feel that we
are too willing to take umbrage at what they say when we have
invited them to speak their minds. When the wind blows, the
successful mentor bends like a reed.

Of course, your class might not begin with resistance and
a sudden need for nimble footwork. If it doesn't, get the workshop started with exercises that are designed to draw the class
together and get the writing flowing. Several of these are listed
under "Exercises for the First Week." (We discuss the role of
the teacher's comments in the next chapter.) In the first week,
the teacher should do everything she can to keep things simple, centering on the positive, on what makes her excited as
someone who enjoys poetry. We need not worry about appear-
ing too simpleminded to our smartest students, as long as we
are creative and supportive in the ways we listen and invite
people in the workshop to converse about what they are hearing. Even the most advanced writers—*especially* the most
advanced writers—crave peer support in order to feel that

their future work, which will be written from the depths of the heart, will be taken seriously. And the more lighthearted students don't want to feel bogged down by seriousness right away, either—they want to see that the workshop is a place to escape the judgments of school and have fun. Striking a flexible balance between seriousness and fun is a productive way to begin the workshop.

At the beginning of the workshop, most critical comments or suggestions for improvement should take a backseat to the necessary task of showing students how to comment on each other's work. Try to find one positive or suggestive detail in every piece you hear. If the poem is funny and everyone is laughing, ask what makes the poem so funny. If the poem is sad, deep, or emotionally taxing, ask what makes it that way. Draw your students into responding to the workshop exercises in terms of the work itself. This is a simple but astoundingly productive practice.

We call this method *detail-hunting*, and it undergirds the way we critique almost every poem in the five weeks of the workshop. Detail-hunting amounts to the following: When we hear or read any poem, we concentrate hard to find at least one conspicuous, interesting aspect of the poem to discuss. We use that significant, salient detail to lead the discussion in the hope that it will help the students think not only about what they like about a peer's poem, but more importantly, about what it was that drew them to admire the poem in the first place.

When we consistently use the detail-hunting method, our students know that we are listening to their work on its own terms and through the lens of the students' own preoccupations. After seeing this method in action again and again, students begin following suit by finding their own favorite details in poems. Our students seem quicker to learn how to point to phrases that catch their ear and suggest interesting possibilities for future writing than they are to learn other forms of critiquing poetry.

Engaging the class in this fashion achieves many things at the outset of the workshop. Not only does it show the poet that her peers are listening to her work, and listening carefully, but it gives writers new ideas for their own writing, ideas such as "every written detail offers an opportunity to make contact with one's audience in a unique way" and "at its root, great writing is concrete."

Suppose a student writes "the sound of spokes" in a sentence describing the way a boy rode a bicycle through a small town. It is easy to teach that this phrase doesn't really explain what the sound was—the way the spokes clicked, their splashing through a puddle, etc. We may wonder aloud: Do spokes even make a sound? Or is it some other part of the bicycle that is making the sound?

By pointing to a detail like this early in the workshop, we can direct our writers to think about sharing *onomatopoetic* moments with their audience—that is, moments in performing their work when they intone the very sound they define. If our student writers are sensitive to this kind of suggestion early in the course, we can draw our own phrasing from the language of opportunity. In other words, we can move from "this phrase could be more specific" to "you've created an opportunity for one of the best descriptions of spokes I've ever seen." When we find moments of potential (for instance, at the level of detail) in an especially vulnerable workshop, our teaching hinges on our own excitement at finding the gem of a startling possibility. These gems exist in almost all pieces of student writing, and give you a wide variety of moments to discuss as the workshop members begin offering their writing in a public forum. The language of opportunity sounds something like this: You've gotten yourself thinking of an evocative image, now it's up to you to take advantage of it by filling in your writing with specific, concrete detail.

Every piece of work raises a subject. In the first week of the workshop, it is your job to find the positive, draw it out before the entire class, and move on. There will be ample time for written criticism later in the workshop.

## Exercises for the First Week

These early exercises are meant to encourage and excite new writers, so the writing they generate should be read aloud to the group and met with as much enthusiasm as we can muster. A good rule of thumb is to discuss at least one aspect or detail of each student's work. The teenagers in a poetry workshop will only begin to offer their peers feedback once they have heard and seen how you, the teacher, respond. This will take pressure off, and provide much needed breathing room as the workshop begins to take over for itself. At the outset, then, you should do your best to remain excited, approving, and eager for anything produced from an exercise. Here are some tried-and-true activities to help you get started.

1. *Dictionary Poem.* Photocopy a dictionary page on which all the words start with the same letter. At random, pull five words off the page and ask the students to freewrite as fast as they can, making sure to include all five words. Have each student read aloud. Students will often employ poetic techniques such as rhyme, assonance, alliteration, and internal rhyme without even knowing it. Your job in this exercise is to pay careful attention to how the students are prone to write. Keep a notebook handy to jot down what you notice. Later in the workshop, the notes will help you see how a student's preoccupations have changed. The notes can also help you design exercises that push your students to new ways of writing.

2. *Exquisite Corpse.* In this exercise, cribbed from the art of the surrealists (who are discussed more fully in Chapter 2), break your students into groups of four or five. Have each group start by putting a piece of paper at each end of the group. Make it clear that the exercise must begin and end with a first-person narrator (the narrative "I"), but that everyone should otherwise write whatever they like. The first student writes two or three lines— no more than thirty seconds' worth of writing—then folds the

paper over all the lines except the bottom one, which serves as a guide for the next writer. The paper is passed to the next student, and the next, until it is full of writing. Each group should write two or three of these poems, keeping at least two going continuously so that everyone is writing as often as possible without feeling rushed. At the end, have the groups read these often profound and even more often hilarious writings to the class as a whole.

*3. List Poem, or the New Year's Resolution.*  Have your students write a poem in the form of a list or running catalog, each line of which begins with the same phrase. The poem will grow more and more powerful as the repetition establishes itself. Start by asking the class to write a New Year's resolution poem that begins "What I will do by the time I am twenty-five." Encourage your writers to stretch their imaginations and avoid the kinds of feats that might be included in a résumé. After all the students have read their poems to the class, direct them to write a second poem, beginning "What I will not do by the time I am twenty-five." (Joe Brainerd's "I Remember" is a fantastic example of this form in action.)

*4. A Generation of Humor.*  Have all your students think of an adult whom everyone in the class knows, then without mentioning the person's name or otherwise being offensive, write a humorous description of the person in such a way that the other students will be able to guess who that person is by the end of the poem. This exercise can work for especially resistant classes because it provides an outlet for minds that want to speak but that need to begin from the outside before they can write from within.

*5. The Language of a Tomato.*  Ask your class to describe a tomato in writing without using the words *tomato*, *red*, or *round* (or *ketchup-producing*!). Read aloud. If it goes exceptionally well, try this exercise describing other things—the sky, a car, music, and so on. This exercise helps students develop a sense of how rich details can be and opens the door for meaningful, concrete discussions of student poems later in the workshop.

**6. *Grant a Wish.*** Have each student write out a wish that has nothing to do with the workshop. The wish should be personal, but also whimsical and silly. It should be brief, with just a few details. The students then fold up the papers and put them in the middle of the circle. Everyone picks up one piece of paper and writes a poem that develops the wish more fully. For example, if the wish is "I want to fly," the poem might explain what the author wants to do once the wish is granted, where she wants to go, and what that place will look like. Read aloud. This exercise is especially helpful for writers who want to share their feelings but who need the shelter of someone else's wish to express themselves.

**7. *Perform Your Name.*** This exercise is designed to begin the process of improving performance, rather than writing, and to give students ideas for their future writing of poems that will be performed. It will work especially well if your group members are comfortable with their own voices but are tired of writing for the moment. The idea is to have students perform their own names exactly as they would sound in a perfect world, with body language being used to help add meaning. This exercise will also help you cultivate how you speak about the way words are performed. Remind everyone that names are used over and over and over again every day in many forms, as a way of calling, as identification. Once your name becomes invested with your personality, you gain the power to *name yourself*.

**8. *Performing a Poem in a Collaborative Setting.*** Set Fridays aside for performing work. Some students will be reluctant to perform their own work the first week, so bring in lots of photocopied poems that are good for collaborative performing. (Try Gwendolyn Brooks' "We Real Cool," e.e. cummings' "he said she said," Nikki Giovanni's "Ego Tripping," and Philip Levine's "They Feed They Lion.") This is an excellent way to build bonds among your writers, especially since they are performing something that everyone has just read for the first time.

**9. *The Performance of a Comedian.*** Show the class a segment of a videotape of a stand-up comedian's routine. As they watch, have them talk about the comedian's body language and tone. Afterward, ask the students to discuss how the body language and tone do or do not enhance the comedian's point. Next, have one or two of the most vocal members of the workshop play the comedian, imitating the performance tools the students saw used in the videotape clip.

**10. *Mimicking Ourselves.*** In this dynamic performance exercise, teacher and students stand in a circle. One person begins by making a noise or a gesture that feels dramatically expressive. The next person mimics that sound or gesture and performs one of her own. The third person mimics the first two, then adds his own noise or gesture. The exercise continues to grow until everyone has gone—or beyond, if students are having a good time trying to remember and perform all the sounds and gestures.

## Leveling the Playing Field

If you've noticed that almost all of the above exercises begin with writing and end with an oral performance for the whole class, you have noticed a crucial strategy in the trajectory of a Youth Speaks workshop. The members of a typical Youth Speaks workshop are diverse—not simply in terms of race, gender, and economic class, but also in terms of education, learning type, and personality. In light of this diversity, many of our teachers begin their workshops by asking the students to indicate by a show of hands whether they are born writers or readers, listeners or speakers. Almost as soon as these questions are asked, we can get a sense of who will initially prefer the performance aspect of the class and who will appreciate its literary aspects. We can also gain an initial sense of who may be challenged by the workshop, and in what ways.

The same workshop may have students who have been accepted at schools like Harvard or Brandeis, and students who have recently been released from probation and who at first have no intentions of going to college. This mixture of students provides a teeming forest of experience for the writing of poetry because it expands the range of experience that all the students can write about and widens the entire workshop's learning curve. We must find teaching methods that do not privilege one kind of experience over another, but that allow all students to contribute to the workshop's pool of poetic and lived experience.

We call this *leveling the playing field*, but in effect what we are doing is providing an intellectual space that rewards all kinds of thinkers. The diversity of thinkers has been described by such different minds as Howard Gardner and Antonio Gramsci, both of whom are inspirations for us as teachers of diverse classrooms and inform the method and thinking behind our workshops.

In *Multiple Intelligences: The Theory in Practice* (1993), Gardner offers a glimpse of what a truly diversified pedagogical method would look like, a method that stems from the deep belief that people have strikingly different ways of learning, many of which are not privileged in the traditional pedagogy of the English classroom. According to Gardner's beliefs, an effective poetry workshop would be one that was open to writers who learn by reading, by looking at images, by working in musical forms, and in other ways. By crafting exercises that reward as many ways of learning as possible, we can improve the poetry of all of our students.

From the angle of politics, our goal is to teach a *neutral value* classroom, if value is to mean anything more than inclusion and mutual respect. Antonio Gramsci diagnoses this fundamental goal as political through and through. For Gramsci, true diversity in education may mean confronting a problem that is at the heart of the educational system: The centers of highest learning have always celebrated the work of the students who best imitate the voices of the powerful, whether in art, math, or science. Education has always been a means for inculcating the values of civil society, and just one kind of culture has typically been the arbiter of what civil society entails—and has held the purse strings.

But why is what Gramsci describes still a problem, given the emphasis put on diversity in our classrooms in the last forty years? The works of students who do not imitate the voice of power and propriety are always in danger of falling through the cracks. More often than not, the students themselves have fallen through the cracks, have never had the opportunity or systematic support they need, or have never desired to imitate the voice of cultural power. As Gramsci writes in *Selections from the Prison Notebooks* (1971), such experiences are never an isolated occurrence:

> The individual consciousness of the overwhelming majority of children reflects social and cultural relations which are different from and antagonistic to those which are represented in the school curricula.(35)

As teachers of poetry at the open door to a students' values, we have a choice: We can try to bend our students' voices to imitate the dominant cultural voice, or we can work with our students to develop their own consciousness, on their own terms.

Lest we (or any of our colleagues) judge that someone who speaks in a voice that we do not recognize as "scholarly" or "learned" is not saying something of intellectual value, we would do well to remember Gramsci's pithy words:

> One cannot speak of non-intellectuals, because non-intellectuals do not exist.(9)

It is for these reasons that we urge high school teachers to mix classes of differing abilities, ages, and experiences when beginning a workshop. Nothing could be more harmful for young writers to see than that only the students with the best grades are rewarded for their efforts. Break the traditional pecking order of the high school classroom in as many ways as possible and you will see that the unfamiliar reigns and sparks immense growth.

(Adult writers would benefit from the same kind of intermingling, wouldn't they?)

We must take special measures to ensure that each workshop proceeds without excluding or privileging certain students on the basis of their performance in school. After all, these workshops are about performing poetry that is of personal and social concern—whatever those words come to mean for our students. They are *not* a surrogate for the debate team, or simply an extension of honor roll, any more than they are a place to escape from demerits and detentions. The workshops are not practice for the SAT or any other standardized test—they are designed to empower everyone and anyone who wants to start writing about their world and begin speaking their minds with sharpened wits and chiseled words.

As a result, we ask *every* student to read aloud. Because we want to protect our most vulnerable students—the ones who are skeptical of the workshop and of the stellar students who eclipse them in high school—and to keep them from worrying about spelling and diction, grammar and literary content, we don't at first push students to hand their work to others. There will be a time for reading each other's work, but that time is not now, at the beginning of the workshop.

Thus, in the beginning, the exercises hinge on assignments that are the product of common experience, and not educational experience. We like to begin with such topics as humor, relationships, and gesture. Later in the workshop we bring in more technical poetic and performative effects, such as rhythm and tone. But for now, the mantra is "no worries," because we know from experience that even our most academically gifted students need to practice and work hard on their performance as much as they need to take a step back and do the honest work of describing situations, scenes, and events.

In the end, we are trying to get our students to become surgeons of their own minds and politicians of their own social positions. Tasks this difficult require much thought, much trust, and, always, much practice.

## A Student Profile and Poem for the First Week

As you read an excerpt from Barnabus Shakur's untitled poem
and the student profile that follows it, consider his work as both
an example of the kinds of students we teach and a model of the
kinds of poems a workshop will produce. Barnabus' life and
writing illuminate each other in many ways. We recommend that
you have your students read his poem and description out loud.

## Excerpt from "Untitled"
### Barnabus Shakur

> I was raised in shades
> Of grays and reds
> Light mixed with abyss and blood
> The mist
> The rains
> The flood
> The pains that came with love
> The things that fired slugs
> Where arguments led to fists
> To sticks, to knives, to guns
>
> I was raised where
> When there was no doh
> Stick a vic then run away
> A chosen few so bold
> They run your doh
> Then walk away
> Where so many lives were lost in the corner
> You'd swear the chalk mark was stain
> In a place where 12 year old men
> Trying to get brain
>
> I was raised where 10 shots meant
> Someone was only grazed
> And 2 meant

In a few days
There'll be a funeral around the way
Where for a quarter
If someone didn't like you
They'd punch you in your face
And snatch your chain
Where helpless women
Sprayed mace in vain
Always doing the wrong things
Swearing you won't do it again

I was raised harshly
In a place where shots never stopped the block party
Fuck it
A place where when it was too hot
The whole block brought out the buckets
The only time you didn't get wet
Was when luck hit
Where a family dinner
Was hot dogs, ketchup, and mustard
And I must say
It would not have been the same
Without Kool-Aid
And there is no shame
I ain't lying
If you don't believe me
Ask me what color it is
One isn't it

I was raised explicit
My life was a past phase
That I lived in
Filled with pains
And visions
When I have children
It'll be their turn to live it

To place Barnabus' poem in a social context, consider this excerpt from a 2001 *Daily News* article titled "2nd Suspect Held in Slay of Teen":

> Police arrested a second suspect yesterday in the Christmas Eve slaying of a Washington Heights teen shot for his gold chain . . . Police said Lopez lives across the street from the place where Juan Melendez, 19, was felled with four bullets from a .40 caliber handgun after turning over his $1,000 gold necklace and religious medallion . . . Melendez was given the gold rope chain and large medallion— bearing the image of St. Barbara, the patron saint of soldiers—by his father, police said. (Weir, R. 2001. "2nd Suspect Held in Slay of Teen." *Daily News*, 17 January, 17)

Barnabus' despairing poem grapples with describing the world as he sees and lives it and with honestly trying to find a way for himself through the dangers and torments of the world. Almost all of the poets in our Youth Speaks workshops deal with issues as serious as these in their writing. In Chapter 3, another of our poets describes trying to forge a way in a world where teens are gunned down for their chains.

---

**Student Profile: Barnabus Shakur**

My name is Barnabus Shakur. I am 19 years old and I recently graduated from William E. Grady High School. For me, Youth Speaks offers a comfortable stress-free atmosphere, which I can't recall High School ever doing. I always had to tip toe. At Youth Speaks I can walk. At Youth Speaks, the "students" do not have to worry about getting a grade. It's their choice to attend the program or not. The environment is not at all a threat, which gives the students space to be themselves and open to say what they feel.

Diversity is one thing I love about Youth Speaks. The differences in culture and personalities that comes with diversity allows our poetry to grow with a unique sense of originality. Being able to hear the opinion of people different only by heritage and sometimes gender will allow a poet to focus on the misunderstandings of his/my poetry.

The first time I felt this program was for me was in the 'summer of 99.' This was when I first came in contact with Youth Speaks, it was at a Teen Poetry Slam. I performed that afternoon and took second place, ever since I've been involved, almost religiously.

High school was a great place for me to be creative, I had to create ways to make money (legally), stay out of trouble (legally), and graduate (legally). High School gave me the opportunity and the social means I needed to use my full salesman potential, and creating the supply for the things that were in demand. I learned in school that it is "the door that squeaks that gets oiled." I graduated from high school not because of merit or bribery, but because of my communication skills.

The opportunity of performing was a great help in strengthening my writing. Feeling the audience's vibes, responses and energy helped me to craft a form of writing that the audience loves and one that leaves a reader bedazzled.

# ▪▪▪ 2 ▪ Generating Momentum

*Watching my students stand up in a large room of people,*
*some of them strangers, I felt that the teen poets [from Youth*
*Speaks] had done something that some teachers don't do for these*
*young people in four years of high school. We watched the*
*students share their own creative gifts and we were amazed*
*at the diversity of talent that we have in our school—*
*talent we always knew existed, but never saw in action.*

—Rebecca Rufo, 9th and 10th grade teacher, Brooklyn, NY

*The fear that cuts off poetry is profound: it plunges us deep, far*
*back to the edge of childhood. Beyond that it does not go.*
*Little children do not have this fear, they trust their emotions. But*
*on the threshold of adolescence the walls are built.*
*Against the assaults of puberty, and in those silvery delicate*
*seasons when all feeling casts about for confirmation. Then, for the*
*first time, you wonder "What should I be feeling?" instead of the*
*true "What do you feel?" "What do I feel? . . .*
*Poetry is written from these depths; in great poetry you feel a*
*source speaking to another source.*

—Muriel Rukeyser (1996, 15–16)

In the second week, we want to improve students' writing and confidence by developing the workshop into that rare gift: an audience that is a community. When the members of a workshop feel like a community, they're interested in hearing each other's poetic voices improve, and they become an audience that strives to know and understand the poet's interactions with them.

24

Spoken-word poetry is always performed before an audience. It draws us together with its immediate, vocal candor. Sometimes it expresses our shared language in a way we have never heard it, demands that we see ourselves and our community in a new light. And at its best, spoken-word poetry rides as high as the poet can take his listeners, as far as he can bond them together for a common end, whatever that may be. In these moments, hearing spoken-word poetry and the vocal responses it elicits from its audience is an electric experience—the experience of feeling poetic energy create a community right before our eyes.

Youth Speaks workshop teachers work hard to give students the feeling that *these writers, in this workshop* represent that sacred, best part of a writer's audience—a community dedicated to improving and applauding each other's work.

As all teachers know, achieving this kind of community is hard work. For as much as teen writers can be excited about writing and performing, they can also be fiercely protective of their writing and nervous and anxious at the possibility of being misinterpreted. By playfully redefining the way the workshop understands the word *meaning*, we can create an atmosphere in which the students bond with each other, listen, and, ultimately, revise their work as a team. Our second job is to construct exercises that are low-risk, community based (or group centered), and what we might call *genius producing*. Since in the second week students are still growing accustomed to each other, it is essential that, even as they generate writing that is of genuine interest and promise, the exercises be playful.

How can we create a community of writers who depend on themselves for improvement and support? One very effective way is to begin the week with a mock contract that all students and the teacher sign. The aim of this contract isn't to hold anything over anyone's head, but simply to highlight that the workshop's members are the most important voice of criticism. A sample contract might read

> As a member of this workshop, I recognize that the
> most effective way to improve my own writing is by
> listening to and striving to help improve the writing
> of the writers around me. The harder I think about
> improving my peers' work, the better I will be at writ-
> ing and performing my own poetry. And the more
> positively I can express what I like and what I want to
> see changed in a poem, the better I will be at listening
> to criticism from my fellow writers—and accepting
> it—as I improve the way I say what I want to say.

If the contract is used to draw students' attention to the importance of listening to one another, it can provide the spark that the
workshop needs to start bonding. The contract will rarely, if ever,
be used again later in the workshop.

A second tool for beginning this week works well for more
developed writers—writers who for one reason or another feel that
their work will not be understood by the workshop. Such writers
can drag the group's motivation and level of discussion down with
their reluctance to add their own work or honest feedback to the
conversation. In a situation like this, a radical move can help: We
ask the class to consider the idea that a poem essentially means
nothing until it is brought to the workshop, read, and discussed. Of
course, this is done with a wink, because every writer knows that
their poem means what they think it means, not what someone else
thinks it means. But if we can pretend for the five weeks of the
workshop that a poem only means something once someone else in
the workshop understands it (especially that smart, quiet writer at
the edge of the circle), we can draw our reluctant writers (and our
excited ones, too) together in a process that depends on careful listening, tinkering, and deep revision. This kind of thinking creates
an atmosphere in which everyone performs, everyone listens, and
everyone comments. Without all of these things happening in the
workshop, the poems that we write are incomplete.

These tools offer two vital ways to make the workshop the
central authority in the classroom, the primary voice for cri-

tiquing and applauding student work. They also spread the responsibility for reading and listening carefully among all members of the workshop. Every reader and listener in the room can thus offer insight to any writer in the class—they, not the poet, hold the meaning to the poem. Under this system, if a writer feels his work has not been understood, he needs to rewrite until he achieves the desired effect—and generating that effect must come about with the workshop's response in mind. The message in class is this: Listening and reworking carefully isn't just a classroom rule, it is the mark of a genuine poet. In the second week, defining meaning in this way helps prepare the workshop members to become each other's smartest, most supportive audience.

By making this community-based definition of *meaning* central, we can help students avoid what might be called the "cult of the misunderstood poet"—a mechanism almost all writers adopt to protect themselves from vulnerability and criticism. Ultimately, "I was misunderstood" only keeps the writer from improving his work in relation to its readers. Since spoken word is literally about communion with the audience, shifting responsibility to the group early can make the later transition to performing poetry in front of large, unfamiliar audiences less daunting. Whatever your teaching style, we hope that you will use the early part of the workshop to structure the class around the students in a way that draws all students to participate in and benefit from the work at hand.

In the second week many Youth Speaks teachers start to forefront the use of positive teacher feedback in relation to the peer comments made about student poems. We make sure to mark moments in the class discussion when positive and helpful comments are made about student writing. This lets us model giving feedback for the students. This kind of metafeedback also reassures student writers that the comments they receive from their peers are important. Teachers may feel more comfortable commenting only on the poems themselves, but using this strategy helps foster the workshop's desire to give more generous feedback. And positive feedback often has an unexpected, equally positive result: It can spur student writers to work harder on their own writing in order to encourage more people to think deeply about their work. The workshop thus not only affords the constructive criticism that's necessary to each writer's improvement, but, if the criticism is slanted in a positive direction, gives the young performers the confidence they need to face unfamiliar audiences with self-possession and wit.

Positive feedback builds on itself in the spoken-word classroom. In the second week, the young writers will be gauging what earns praise in the workshop at the level of writing and criticism. At this early stage, be cautious with criticism: One truly negative comment too early in the workshop may outweigh five positive ones.

In the second week of the workshop, then, we develop upon the community building of the first week by using exercises that foster a common purpose and respect among the student writers. The students' individual writing skills cannot be fully expanded until each student feels that the workshop members have formed a working, supportive audience and community.

## Community Building the Group Way

Many of our teachers like to begin the second week's community building by directing a discussion about what it means to be young, about the terms, accomplishments, and challenges this generation faces. Not until answering these generational questions can we as teachers recognize and celebrate the specific differences that this generation of writers presents to us.

After finishing a student-based exercise in the first week of a workshop, one of our teachers heard a piece that reminded him of Gil Scot-Heron's "Pardon our Analysis (We Beg Your Pardon)," a performance piece in which Scot-Heron explores the political and social problems of the Watergate era. The teacher played the compact disc in the next workshop, then led a discussion on the similarities and differences between Scot-

Heron's 1973 and the students' feelings about social conditions in the year 2000. Although the workshop had just begun, the students were quicker to point out the *poetic* and *performative* differences between themselves and Scot-Heron than major social and political ones. What we have found, again and again, is striking: Our young poets, more influenced by musical culture than ever, have a firmer sense of stylistic differences as a marker of their generation than perhaps any other poetic feature. They are unusually adept at speaking of *meter*, *alliteration*, and *tone* (among other poetic features) when they talk about what tends to interest them most—their musical culture.

Marking stylistic differences is an excellent place to begin thinking about what it means to be a poet. It allows workshop members to begin thinking about their stylistic differences and to assess how their peers approach the writing process. This exercise also evidences the necessity of filling each class with as many *performed* writing exercises as possible—for not only are the individual's writing and performance taken seriously by the entire workshop, but the students' ability to hear and catalog their peers' work is improved as well.

Consider the poem "Hip Hop," written by Morgan Cousins, a member of Youth Speaks since 1999 and a 2000 NYC National Teen Slam Team member. Morgan describes the very issues that we ask ourselves to prompt through discussions and exercises. Read her poem and the student profile that follows it to your workshop to foster even deeper discussions about the issues that pertain directly to today's youth.

## Hip Hop
**Morgan Cousins**

> Hip Hop must die to
> Be reborn in the
> New millennium
> Cause everyone's tired
> Of the same old idioms

Mixed on new beats
Or new beats and
Dum-dums on baby
Teeth

We had french vanilla,
Butter pecan, to the
Peta-ricans. From
The "brrr's" of pigeons
To unfaithful women
Who called themselves
Widows cause suburban
Doors could breathe

Minds of so called
Prodigies remained
Blunted and stunted
Cause that's how hits were made
We had Machiavelli
Rebirth of history
2000, millennium, and end of days

self destruction went
through convulsions
and transformed our cities
our urban suburban ghetto
societies
which painted the impenetrable
picture of who we should be
we rocked gold chains to
big clocks and now
blue diamond rocks
symbolizing our
superficial status
as we continuously fail
to hear cries of Hawaiian Sophie
Carters dying

cause of lack of Christ

Hip hop, oh this hip hop culture
That changed from self worth
Is now self murder
We rocked Pumas to tims
Girbaud to Iceberg
But blunts stayed the same
As our hip hop culture
Slowly fused together with the
Crack game

You've gone from
Poppin' cheeks to Casio beats
While heads bopped
Extemporaneously
You made vocabulary
Incoherent phrases of
Mixed tenses, and brick fences so we
Could not escape

By way of Spiga
You've released a
Money hungry,
Food secondary;
Spawn
Created fiends
Hungry for names
Unable to pay
To fill their
Maw

I think you've got me
Singing the blues
Got fools looking for the
Red stripe on the heels
Of shoes
Made us proud of project

Wars
While we lived in worlds
With no doors
As you became the only
Future
Raped us, turned
Us into new creatures
Into the best
Non-paid advertisers,
She rocks Gucci on
Her coochie, but
Gucci's not paying her
Hung those nooses
Round our necks
As we became
Platinum flaunters
In the projects

You threw my independence
Out the door
Called me bitch
Gold digger
Money sexer
15 minute diggin' pleasure
non-provider
dick rider
baby father havin'
diamond ring rockin'
giving that ass
low class to no cash
pigeon, chicken
the mistress, the ghetto
princess

I don't want a record deal
Cause I can't spit
Rabid spiel

And then preach
God when I'm done
Perform rehearsed
Spiritual factors when
I've won the prize
The prize of Africa
But not sure where I went
It's not a country
It's a continent

Not looking for the talent
I've got
Looking for the hardest
Dick
The loosest twat
The who can
Spit a verse that
Don't mean squat
"nah mean" em and
awe, like they've never
been taught
walk around bustin'
shots, wavin' a Rolex
watch and swear it's
fame they got
and that
cross they rock,
God knows them not

It's you. You, the gaudy seed-bearer,
The hardship hearer, the music maker,
The death bringer, ears ringer
Soul shaker, movie maker
Unity sayer
You take lies,
And manifest them into
Devilish dreams

That seem like what is
Wanted
As words lay spoken
We are named token
Hopes stay broken

Oh hip hop,
Where did your love go?
You who preach this unity
Purely for show.

---

**Student Profile: Morgan Cousins**

I came up with the idea of "Hip Hop," when I was walking down Prince Street. There was a sticker that said hip hop must die . . . and then a few feet later I saw a sticker that said the new millenium. I then took those two ideas and incorporated them together to create the first line for the poem. But that's all I had, a first line. What that first line did for me was made me start thinking about what were the defects within hip hop. Hip hop had taken the world by storm, and had become a whole culture by itself. Which made me a little irate about the fact that it was slowly losing its fire, and becoming extremely commercialized. I started writing it, and then put it down for about three months because I was completely stuck on where to go with it.

When I joined Youth Speaks I was completely not who I am today. There were traces of the me today there, but I had not yet grown into myself as a writer. Going to the classes made me gain confidence in my writing, and then slowly improve on it. When I first performed, I think that was my biggest problem. I hadn't learned how to be confident. I was much too worried about being a crowd-pleaser, than being a good writer. That's what I most appreciate about the program. Youth Speaks allows us to all be writers first, and performers next. This is the most crucial part about spoken word, for me at least. Well, actually, if you have the balance of both things, writing and performing, that's even better.

I realize now, more than any other point in writing, that I am a talented writer. And I owe some of this to Youth Speaks. I have been writing for 5 years, and I have so much to improve on. Writing is a never-ending process, and I am just loving it continually . . .

Discuss how Morgan's student profile relates to the poem "Hip Hop" and wonder aloud how stylistic differences affect the poem's meaning—how a poem is written, read, and performed enhance what the poem is trying to say. Ask several students to read sections of the poem aloud, in different ways, until it reaches a maximal effect—the one reading that feels the most powerful, moving, evocative. Raise other questions: What makes Morgan's style different from the styles of students in the class who are writing about the same thing? How is each student's style effective in getting their point across? How does Morgan express an issue with her own uniqueness—an issue that is urgent and interesting to the workshop as a group of young writers? These questions will be fruitful not because they will necessarily be answered at such an early stage in the workshop, but because they will help student writers define their own niches—while they are thinking about differences between other students' work, they will also start thinking about what makes their own work different from everybody else's. They will also begin taking up the topic of style in their poetry, and think about how it can be used to further develop their work. The last question is rewarding because it further reduces the scope of the teacher's presence in the class because it is simply a question he cannot answer. The teacher is never the purveyor of cool. Making the young writers in the class the "experts" further gives the authority to the group—of the workshop itself.

If these questions lead to a particularly robust discussion, ask these questions: What topics need to be written about from a youth perspective? Is there a particular style that is most suited for youth poets, a style that embodies "cool"? What is it, and why is it a youth form?

If one thing characterizes the Youth Speaks program in this respect, it is that our teachers are willing to listen to teen writers with teen concerns. Healthy questioning of students' views is appropriate and encouraged, but it is the students' own estimation of their generation that is ultimately important.

Granting authority to the entire workshop group does not diminish our role as teachers. Instead, it lets us shift our attention toward students who are in danger of being left behind in the solidifying community. Teachers in spoken-word workshops must be particularly aware of students who express views or use poetic forms that are outside the fold of what the workshop is producing—writers who, because of lifestyle or artistic temperament, choose to create in a solitary aesthetic niche. Instead of drawing attention to the differences between their work and the other students', move the discussion forward by focusing on what the workshop members like and admire about these students' pieces. We want to do everything we can to keep any writer from feeling ostracized. The more connections we can make in the workshop as we lead discussions, the more these peripheral writers will feel comfortable creating and offering honest feedback—feedback that is often as quirky, useful, and surprising as their work.

The process of community building inevitably leaves a few students behind. We teachers must acknowledge who these students are and work naturally to give them the feedback they are asking for—whether or not they know they are asking for it.

One high school student who might have been left behind in the workshop community was Aaron Lutz-Kinoy, a member of the 2000 NYC Youth Speaks National Teen Slam Team who now attends the State University of New York at Purchase. Before he became an accomplished poet, Aaron was self-described (not without tongue in cheek) as inhabiting "the bottom of the food chain" at his high school. After several visits to the principal and flunking his classes, he may have slipped through the cracks altogether. But, as a few of his teachers recognized, Aaron was burning with the desire to express himself. Aaron's student profile gives an account of his high school experience: what he did not get from the traditional classroom, what he found at Youth Speaks, and how he eventually found his own poetic voice and earned the positive feedback he needed to continue pushing his writing to higher and higher levels.

### Student Profile: Aaron Lutz-Kinoy

As far back as my mushy memory can remember, I have always disliked school. The restrictive nature of the traditional classroom, the typical age divisions, uniform standards of learning and social hierarchies and Aaron never really clicked. After a year at the local grade school, PS 139 in Flatbush, New York, I attended Brooklyn Friends School in downtown Brooklyn for eight years. Having virtually no friends at the place, I developed a nervous condition of inability to unearth the courage to speak in groups of more than four or five people. I was a mess. Scrawny and pimple riddled, hiding behind bangs, even if I knew an answer in class, my arm would fall into an indecisive half-mast.

In my shell, I began writing stories and poems.

Frustrated and dwelling among the bottom of the food chain, I fought kids and got sent to the infamous office a lot. My first opportunity for publication was a classy little magazine that the middle-school was putting together. The poem was a trite satirical piece about fencing. Founded by a handful of wealthy

Quakers, the institution wished to cut out a line about a gun. I argued as best an idealistic little kid could about how much our families are paying for our education here. "Freedom of speech . . . This is a democracy!"

"No, this is not."

They left my piece out.

My grades had been pretty shitty for some time, but whenever I put the least bit of effort into English class, I excelled. Finding something academic that I was good at was nice. I felt confident that, still a depressed underachieving geek, I was definitely not dumb.

The next year, I started from scratch at School for the Physical City, a small "alternative" public high-school experiment, founded on ideals and a couple of real quality teachers. Although there were a slew of problems outside of school and internal family matters, the next four years were a piece of cake. I failed maybe one class the whole time. My aggressive rabble-rousing had expanded to the larger social issues, the stuff revolutions and great poems are built upon.

One day, wading through the lifeless muck of a high school creative writing class, we were joined by an impressive young woman who showed us a video of slam poetry. As soon as I saw the stuff I wanted in. The teacher of the class, Marc Barnhill had specifically asked her to speak with me after her presentation. Jen was offering free after-school poetry and creative writing workshops due to start in a couple of weeks. I was sold, enrolled and soon a regular at Youth Speaks. The weekly word play went down at 14th Street, housed in Teachers and Writers Collaborative. I had never had something like this. Of course, there had been a couple of incredible teachers along the way who had individually boosted my confidence a bit, but no formal classroom compared to the environment created by Youth Speaks. Somehow they built a structured space where young people felt free to speak. The interest in writing served as a common ground on which, whether you liked your peers or not, you respected them and you respected the mentors, because they were doing the same thing we were. In being taught by excellent teachers and fellow poets there was a sense that they were learning and building as well.

Probably the best free-writing exercises were accomplished when the mentors would take part in the exercise too. One felt like there was a constant exchange like we were mutating into one multi-faceted fleshy organism climbing to better writing. This synergy had never ever occurred in a school classroom.

Which brings us to the Slam. For those who still do not know, a poetry slam is like any other performance of poetry but with judges who competitively score the pieces. Like any competition there are the inevitable winners and losers. Sometimes there are team Slams, in which one team of poets competes against another. In April of last year [2000], after placing our way through a series of these slams, I, and five other individuals, formed a New York team and took our sleeping bags out west to hilly San Francisco to compete in the second annual National Youth Slam. It was probably the most soul baring, mind-boggling work of human expression that I have ever witnessed.

There is so much to be done. I feel like I have abandoned the ship in that this is the first thing I have actually contributed to the program since I left for the State University of New York's Purchase College, last fall. I suppose that is one of the goals of the program, to see kids make it on to better places.

What was it about Aaron's work that caused him to feel so ostracized, and how did Youth Speaks provide a space in which he felt comfortable creating and polishing his craft? Aaron's poetry is bred from the streets of his neighborhood in Brooklyn. It is charged with vernacular language, and informed by a keen eye for detail and rhythm. It is unapologetically honest about its sometimes shocking content—the content that Aaron believes led to his work sometimes being shunned in school. At the same time, Aaron's work is suffused with an awareness of his political positions, a sharp sense of right and wrong, and an often mesmerizing knowledge of the way poetic writing can lend itself to inspired and surprising performances—for Aaron's poetry is, above all, astonishingly performed.

If we are teaching in a school that is concerned about the propriety of a poem's language and content, we may be in a bind if we want to discuss how poetry can be incredibly effective and stirring even if its content is controversial. Consider this excerpt from Aaron's poem "The Same Muthafuckas":

## Excerpt from "The Same Muthafuckas"
### Aaron Lutz-Kinoy

> Ebadading ding ding
> Ebadading ding ding
> Will not go back there again
> Confused teenage nostrils stuffed with ritilin
> From the mind to the beat to the pen to the rant
> I wanna clap holes through pigmobiles as they're
>     driving through my house
> Set up a big rat trap and fucking kill Mickey Mouse
> Turn Steam Boat Willy from black and white to red
> Beat Goofy with a spiked bat while Minny is giving me
>     head
> Slave labor racket hittin all four corners of NAFTA
> Kickin Donald down the elevator shaft

Cuz I have to
Come on! Yellow, red, black, white and brown
All kids living and dying in sweat shops worse than
    Chinatown
Whatever faction you're from and
Rock this joint like an atomic slum
Ebadading ding ding
Ebadading ding ding

Back in your corners the round beginnings
It's the agenda pumpers pimpin voters like whores
Cold to the core
Leaving bruises and sores
Scores of pigs cross the city
Rudy the snitch, about to get ousted by the first witch
We just been sorry for her since her man got his dill
    licked
The talk is strangely changing
With actions always the same
Fuck freedom for the poor
It's like the one party system
Like Bush vs. Al Gore
Just awaiting for the riot
Why you playing us for suckers
The democrats and the republicans work for the same
    muthafuckas
It's an abundant abuse of power that makes me stagger
    and rhyme slow
Swerving round the social organism left loopholes in
    the road
A handful own everything
Constitution confusion
Who but a criminal gives million dollar contributions
So fuck it.
I'm buzzing like a jet carrying bombs that sting

GE like Don King working both sides of the ring
Watching opponents trip on each other
Stumble and slap one
Another k.o. finds
Ain't nothing changing but the headlines
Ebadading ding ding ding
Ebadading ding ding ding

As early as the second week, we need to prioritize what we aim to teach in our workshop. A student like Aaron—a writer who has an intense need to voice himself in political, social, and artistic arenas, no matter how local and specific those arenas are, yet who expresses himself with the power and urgency of real, idiomatic, youth-inspired language—is a gift. Giving a writer like this enough freedom to express himself is risky, but the rewards are potentially immense: As other students in the workshop see that this writer's voice is heard and even celebrated for its poetic richness, we can draw all the workshop members together to improve the details and effectiveness of their own writing.

When he wrote "The Same Muthafuckas," Aaron was eighteen years old. As he matured as a writer, he came to construct poems that were almost as traditional and heartfelt as any sonnet. Never underestimate the importance of accepting your writers' voices and making a commitment to improve their range, sharpness, and effect. For another poem will inevitably follow this one, and another after that. Given how rapidly teenagers can change both the style and content of their writing, we have no idea what gems may lie waiting around the corner.

Consider a poem that Aaron wrote this year for his girlfriend, who is attending college many miles away from him. In it he combines his social and poetic concerns, reworking the traditional tropes and figures of the love poem until they feel like his own.

## Untitled
### Aaron Lutz-Kinoy

> Off the shores where nature gets traded for rivers of
>     green
> four cornered spiritual Mohegan blood still gleams
> on the rocks of the blunts
> or the clay of the bluffs
> we bring the bold mind set of the city to rural streets
> edge of the cliff
> get high
> dabble in indian myth
> my urban wood nymph
> ohio bound
> never forget the sound of your breath in the night
> so take flight fight
> for a fraction of this life that you can hold to
> long as your heart thumps
> I'll catch an echo off the moon and roll through

When you consider a student like Aaron, think in terms of a version of Pascal's wager: What could the workshop gain by accepting this student's voice, by asking about and commenting on his content and language—and what would we lose by quickly shutting him down, maybe before he realizes the range of what he can achieve as a writer?

## *Watching* Poetic License *and Exercise Crafting*

In the second week of the workshop we implement three basic strategies for drawing the class together: We screen *Poetic License* and discuss a set of related questions, community building around the subject of youth, surrealist exercises and the low-risk group poem.

*Poetic License* is a 60-minute documentary on spoken-word poetry available as a supplement to this book. Watching the video widens students' sense of just what qualifies as a poem, which helps us not only to connect our writers with a common generational bond, but also to achieve a richness and uniqueness of expression this week. It gets our students' minds working, perhaps even before they have written anything of substance down. Not only do we hope to show students that the workshop will respect their deepest, most serious thoughts, we also want to let them know that whatever form those thoughts take, they can be rendered into a poem performed for an audience. In our experience, both of these goals can be achieved at the same time.

After screening the movie, ask these questions to begin a discussion of what it means to be a young poet:

- Besides the fact that all of the poets in the video are young, what similarities do they share?
- Who is your favorite poet in the film, and why?
- What about this film helped you learn something about poetry and what it means to be a poet?

In this second week of the workshop, we want our students to be absolutely familiar with certain basic topics—what it means to be a young poet, what it means to be a part of a generation, what particular pressures they feel as members of this group, and so on. We want to think and talk about building, accumulating, and growing. Group freewriting and suppressing the editorial drive are our greatest tools at this point because they help our students to keep the pen on the paper, thinking and writing about their commonalities as young writers. We will think later about pruning or modifying their work, but first the work must be written and the students must grow comfortable with performing in front of the teacher and their peers. Studying the surrealists and their American counterparts, the Beats, is a rewarding way to do this.

## The Surrealists and Spoken-Word Poetry

The term *surreal* has come to denote something that escapes explanation, an event that isn't so much miraculous as it is uncanny, wholly unexpected, and bizarre. In its earliest stages, the surrealist movement depended on a sense of uncanniness for its artistic weight. Such writers and artists as Guillaume Apollinaire, André Breton, René Magritte, and Salvador Dalí thought that the unconscious held the secret to political, social, and aesthetic insight. Through mining media images and text, combining artistic images across genres and traditions, they sought to have their art resonate not with the studied, precise art of the canonical schools, but with the very tangled stuff of the inner mind. Often arresting, obscure, and shocking, their work has come to stand for creativity, spontaneity, and that essential element of all great art, surprise.

At this early stage of the workshop, we want the students to know that there is a school of writers and artists who believe the world is separated into two levels: the world of the accepted (the "real" and canonized), of rules and constraints, of advertising language and newspaper stories; and the colorful world of art and literature, of dreams and the unconscious.

The surrealists found their own dreamlike meanings in the everyday world by cutting up newspapers, by changing the ways people and figures were painted, and by writing as much as they possibly could without the intervention of the rational mind. They created first, and only later modified and polished their work. An especially informative description of the preoccupations of the surrealists can be found in *Surreal Lives*, a biography of André Breton by Ruth Brandon (1999). Brandon describes the surrealist school as originating from Apollinaire:

> Many of Surrealism's icons and technique were originally Apollinaire's. Its pantheon of Sade, Baudelaire, Rimbaud, Jarry (though Lautreamont, the remaining member of this firmament, was their own discovery),

its interest in dreams and chance, its abandonment of
"artistic" subjects in favor of the everyday, its icono-
clasm, its inclusion under one net of both written and
visual arts—all these were inherited from him. (34)

How can we take advantage of this rich art form so early in our
workshop? What about surrealism is especially suited for workshop members who are unfamiliar with considering themselves
as poets?

First, using the surrealists' insistence on spontaneity and its
marked attempt to leave schooling behind gives students a way to
escape writer's block. Second, using exercises based on surrealism
can create an atmosphere where creativity is not judged as being
right or wrong, the way intelligence is. When we describe or listen
to a dream, we suspend our everyday judgment of what a story or
a real event should be; we simply listen, and enjoy something new
and usually quite unexpected. The same kind of effect can be experienced in the workshop, because such a nonjudgmental environment makes writers and listeners feel safe about tinkering with the
way they normally approach their writing.

The surrealists' counterparts in America, the Beats, charged
surrealism with the spontaneity and improvisation of America's
greatest contribution to world art—jazz. Beat writers including
Jack Kerouac, Allen Ginsberg, Diane DiPrima, Anne Waldman,
and William Burroughs privileged freewriting and freedom of
speech over the labored, deeply conceptual writings of the mod-
ernists. (For more on the Beats, refer to *Poetic License*, which
speaks to the Beats' contributions to today's spoken-word poetry.)
Further, they took the social awareness of Walt Whitman, John
Dos Passos and Sherwood Anderson and vivified it with the
rhythms and freshness of their generation.

It's clear why these two similar schools are so useful to
teaching spoken-word poetry: Not only do they offer a form that
can resonate with audiences upon first hearing, but they privilege writing exercises that develop *here* and *now,* and use the collective work of the class as a starting point for poetry that can be

profound without being totally clear or painstakingly wrought. For a workshop that will meet for only five weeks, then, looking at the surrealists and the Beats offers an entertaining way to generate low-risk material, because freewriting gives students who feel vulnerable about showing their work the protective awning of a time limit.

Beginning to write and read social situations in new ways, becoming a reader of the world, seeing relationships in the way people treat each other just as we see relationships between poems and stories—this is one of the first, best moments in maturing as a poet and a thinker. Focusing on freewriting and the thought-expanding tools of the surrealists can help our students make connections and understand those connections as the unifying stuff of great poetry.

The exercises in this chapter are low-risk and what we might call *genius producing*—they often result in brilliant insights that come out of nowhere in a flash. Nothing feels better to a student than to hear someone say, "You wrote *that* in a minute and a half? Think what you can do in an hour!"

We have used this exercise in Youth Speaks workshops:

> In the next five minutes, write the one dream that you cannot forget, no matter how crazy it seems. Don't worry about being poetic or eloquent, simply pay as much attention to the specific details of your dream as you can—what you see, what you hear, how you feel, and so on. Tell the scene of your dream as though it were occurring right in front of you.

Many incredible student writings emerged from this exercise, generating a wonderful discussion about the power of our minds when we aren't *trying* to write anything amazing at all—when we are simply attuned to and honest about how we are reacting to our lives, both awake and asleep. One piece of writing struck us with its beauty and insight. Justine Caccamo wrote the following poem in just two and a half minutes in response to the exercise:

## Untitled

**Justine Caccamo**

The sky was broken and swollen that day, like a deep purple bruise. I don't remember whether or not I'd willed myself there that afternoon or whether I had been brought there and left to my father's empty house. All I remember is that I wanted the heavens to open up and somehow swallow me whole, as if by mingling with sheer void I could overcome its terrible emptiness. And I don't know how long Laura had been standing there behind the glass door for a matter of minutes or for hours on end. I watched the hazel flame that illuminated her frame, set against the storm, from inside. With my hands pressed up against the glass, I felt the cold from the rain as it cut the blazing tropical heat and isolated me from what was outside. The water rained down on me through the cracks in my father's broken ceiling. It trickled inside, tracing cold clear paths in the vapor that formed on the door—dripped down my fingertips, onto my arms, past my elbows, where drop by drop, it pooled on the floor. That night, as I stepped outside, I felt the rain and the cold and Laura, like velvet, as we slipped away into the folds of a darkened fantasy. And that was enough for me to feel.

Justine's dream poem is an example of what can result from a genius-producing exercise, if only because in two and a half minutes (she spent the rest of the exercise time staring into space), Justine was able to create without editing herself, to write without letting the standard of "what a poem needs to look like" crush her creativity before she could express herself. We can't imagine that many lengthy take-home creative-writing assignments would result in work with more urgency and beauty, and such a truly unique and controlled mood.

**Student Profile: Justine Caccamo**

I attend Staten Island Technical High School. I am 16 (undecided but plan on attending a liberal arts program) and one day, I hope to write professionally.

Youth Speaks is a dream. I come from an engineering high school where the humanities department is virtually nonexistent. There is no opportunity for performance, and English classes focus mostly on the mechanics of writing rather than the art. I have found the freedom of creativity this organization offers to be critical in the development of my writing, and in this way it offers me what school cannot.

## Exercises for the Second Week

These exercises for the second week are designed not only to bring the class together as a community of writers united under an umbrella of similar interests, but also to produce effective, detail-based writing on the spot, without students' experiencing the vulnerability that can come from showing work that has been weeks in the making.

*1. Writing to the Beats: Freewriting from the Non-Editorializing Mind.* Begin class by asking everyone to freewrite as fast as they possibly can for five minutes. Make it clear that they should not have any plan for what they are going to write—they should simply write until they stumble upon something that catches their poetic attention. They can write whatever they want—garble, even—*as long as their pens don't stop moving*. After five minutes, ask the students to fold up those pieces of paper and put them away, then pull out a fresh piece of paper. Now ask them to try to write the exact same thing they just wrote for five more minutes—so long as the entire piece is about that thing which they found interesting in the first piece. To facilitate the exercise, make it clear that you are interested in expanding the way their writing changes on-the-spot. This exercise provides the grounds for a discussion on the role of freewriting in finding new and intriguing subjects to write about, and on how useful writing from the non-editorializing mind can be.

2. *The Scene Is in the Seen.* Put students in groups of three or so and have them tear out words they like, notice, or choose arbitrarily from a newspaper. Ask them to decide how to arrange the words to create an *image poem*—a poem that conveys an image, as if drawing a picture with words. Have them add sentences as a group until the poem coheres enough to read aloud. After the group has read the work, they should show the class the way the poem looks with the words taped on the picture. This is a fun exercise for community building.

3. *Beatnik Café: The Birth of the Cool.* Bring in a piece of music without words, at least five minutes long and with a rhythmic, idiosyncratic sound (African, electronica, etc.). Don't be afraid to challenge your workshop members with something that jars them—whether you think that might be Charles Mingus and Eric Dolphy, Glen Miller and Louis Armstrong, Gustave Mahler and Erik Satie (his *Six Gnossiennes* often elicits fantastic responses). Students need to have notebooks and pen ready. When the song plays, they should close their eyes and write whatever they hear, whatever the music tells them—as long as they are writing from within themselves and their experience of the music, and not just what they think the song is supposed to mean. Then have everyone read their work aloud while you replay the same music. Let the exercise prompt a discussion on mood, and on how listening to different kinds of music can provoke radically different kinds of poems.

4. *Is the Story in the Substance or in the Saying?* For this performance-based exercise, have everyone in the workshop form a circle then pick a character and try to tell the simplest of stories—just a few lines long—from that character's perspective. Possible characters

include a subway conductor who is upset about a passenger who became ill on his car, and a mother who is laughing about how her daughter always lies about why she comes home late from school. The only requirement is that students tell their story *in character*, in a different accent or voice. After the performances, talk about how the way we say things can affect the meaning of what is said—sometimes radically so. Ask a student to perform someone else's poem in the voice of a person from another economic class or another race, or simply in a different tone. Then ask the class what using different voices might mean for performing our own poetry. This exercise works well to bring levity to a class that has written too much for the day or that is abnormally restless—it's a high-energy exercise that usually brings a healthy dose of laughter.

5. *Howl for the New Millennium.* Ask every student to begin a poem with something they think must die and be reborn: for example, "Hip-Hop Must Die (to be reborn . . .)." The subject of the poem can be anything but a person. Have the students continue writing off of this subject, with every line being a manifestation of what must die or why. The rest of the poem should explain the first line, and as the poem expands, the students should answer the question *why must it die* in terms of their own experience. This exercise promotes students' awareness of how they relate to the everyday world of mass media culture, neighborhood problems, etc.—whatever issues are pressing for them at the time.

6. *Who Is the Subject?* Pair up your students and send them outside for ten minutes. In the first five minutes, one of them should try to find an object and start writing about it in the most intricate, specific detail possible. The partner watches the writer at work and describes what he sees about his partner as she's writing. After five minutes, the partners switch roles, find a new object, and so on. When everyone comes back into the room, have each pair swap descriptions and try to write a poem that

combines the descriptions of self and of object. After the students read these poems aloud, the discussion will hinge on what it looks like to write about a writer—specifically, how we can generate drama or urgency by using a "view from above."

*7. What Is a Miracle?* Have students read either a dictionary definition of *miracle* or Julio Cortazar's "A Very Real Story" (from *Cronopios and Famas*), or watch the section of Quentin Tarantino's *Pulp Fiction* in which John Travolta and Samuel Jackson argue about what a miracle means. After reading or watching, ask the students to talk about what *miracle* means to them. Does a miracle always have to be good? Could there be a bad miracle? Why? Have them write a poem about a miracle they may or may not have experienced, according to what they think the word *miracle* really means.

*8. Telling Stories from Paintings.* Bring in photocopies of a surrealist painting (Dalí, Magritte, Man Ray). Begin by directing your students to ask questions about only the objects they can see in the painting. (What is that elephant doing standing there? Why is the sun purple? What is that in the far right corner?) After a minute or two, have them try to describe the entire scene, including the single hidden detail that engages them and that perhaps only they can see. Finally, ask your poets to tell a story about themselves in relation to that single object or detail, placing them in the mood, scene, or drama presented by the painting.

*9. Is This Newspaper a Poem?* Bring a bunch of newspapers, scissors, and glue to class. Have the students cluster in groups of three, then cut and paste words and phrases until they have reconfigured the language of advertising into a poem. Then have them give these *found poems* titles at random from articles in the newspaper (the title may or may not explain the poem's theme). Have each group read its poem aloud. (The appendix includes one such found poem.) This is an excellent, low-risk exercise for writers who need to get used to each other as peers.

**10.** *My Gesture Is Our Gesture.* The class needs a wide space in the classroom for this performance-based exercise. (If weather permits, do it outside.) Have the group form a circle. One person steps forward and offers a gesture—a deep breath, a foot-stomp, a hand signal, whatever. The rest of the group repeats the leader's gesture several times, until the leader points at another person in the group. The leader then steps back into the circle and the new leader comes forward to direct the group with a gesture of her own. After a few attempts, your writers will realize that watching an entire group perform the same gesture offers fun and diverse possibilities for performance.

# week ■■■ 3 ■ Using Rhythm and Hip-Hop

*And hopefully . . . hip-hop will openly accept the love I'm pourin in.*
*Take my positive energy and begin flourishin, movin forward and*
*become somethin beautiful*
*So thoughts like mine won't seem so unusual*

—Anthony K-Swift Scott, 18

*If bebop was a response to the wackness of watered down jazz*
*(read: swing), then hip-hop was a response to the wackness*
*of watered down soul (read: disco). And, too, hip-hop's gritty*
*urban birth was a reaction to the deferred dreams of the Civil*
*Rights era . . . In a nation which still has deep racial divisions,*
*hip-hop has become the great cultural bridge.*

—Kevin Powell (1999, 33)

No cultural source has influenced young spoken-word poets more than hip-hop, a musical form rooted in the traditions of rap and the blues. K-Swift (Anthony Maurice Scott, Jr.) is one such poet. He was eighteen when he approached Youth Speaks for the first time during a summer open mic poetry event. One of our teachers knew K-Swift wanted to perform his writing that day, but he hesitated before agreeing to climb the stage. He felt he needed someone to accompany him with a rhythmic "beat box." More than that, he insisted that *if* he were to perform, he needed to be introduced as a rapper—*not* as a poet.

What did K-Swift's hesitation amount to? As teachers of youth poetry know, the resistance of young writers is often linked to a deeply negative association with the word *poetry*. By the third week of our spoken-word poetry workshop, we want to have created a writing classroom that dodges this potential problem.

By this time—the midpoint of the workshop—the students will have grown familiar with themselves as a collection of poets and the teachers will have begun to recognize patterns and styles, performative techniques, and poetic taste. Students are likely to be writing the poem they will perform in three weeks' time. This is the point to make a crucial decision: to push the workshop's writing and performance forward by framing class around the writing, music, and language that our students bring to us, thus creating a group that defines the term *poetry* for itself. Since students may have a very different idea of poetry than teachers do, this method of teaching asks instructors to be very flexible in understanding what an effective poem looks like.

As we work to improve students' writing, we ask, What does each student's poetry remind us of, and how can we bring that source into the classroom for the benefit of the whole workshop? As teachers, we should first turn to our students' writing (whenever it is possible) to draw the workshop into discussions of poetic technique, and only secondarily use sources from outside the classroom.

We also use the third week of the workshop to begin the teaching of deep poetic reading, which we do with the work of our most gifted students. To replicate that kind of classroom work, this chapter analyzes one of K-Swift's earliest Youth Speaks poems.

This chapter provides tools for understanding hip-hop as a complicated poetic form, for conducting deep reading in the class, and for introducing technical poetic devices to students without disinfecting their poetry of inspiration or fun.

In the third week, the teacher's job is to expand and polish the work the students are beginning to perform. The sooner you can learn what the term *poetry* means to your students, the sooner you can begin to coach them to write productively in whatever mode they choose.

## *Turning to Hip-Hop*

Why turn to hip-hop at this stage? Hip-hop is *the* predominant language of urban American youth—it informs their aesthetic culture and it is their dominant mode of expression when they first begin to write. If we use hip-hop in the same way we used the surrealists, we leave the door open for an incredibly rich variety of youth poetry. Our goal, after all, is to make every writer in the workshop comfortable and excited about developing her own voice.

What is hip-hop? We can answer this question indirectly by talking about what it is *not*. To begin, *hip-hop* isn't just a musical term: The word actually refers to a group of related art forms: music (emceeing, deejaying), visual art (graffiti), dance (breaking), and a highly rhythmic and rhymed poetry (rap). Originating in the Bronx borough of New York in the late 1970s, this cultural form spread across urban America and now represents communities as distinct from each other as rural Florida is from suburban Michigan. But though hip-hop has grown to represent more than the urban experience, its core remains the same: Hip-hop culture almost always celebrates the voices of economically and politically disenfranchised communities. As an art form, hip-hop balances the need for social change with the need to entertain and unite community members around a common joy.

For many urban teens, writing and performing hip-hop doesn't simply offer a method for speaking poetically, it offers a prized means of identification that signifies the writer's lifestyle and attendant set of values. This identification functions as both an aesthetic expression and a vocalization of political and social self-awareness. Hip-hop offers young writers an emblem of joy, a sense of protection, a rallying cry in a tough world.

Since so many English classes ignore or shun hip-hop and other vernacular poetic forms, your appreciation and encouragement of hip-hop will signify something immense to your class— and it will help your students feel safe enough to express themselves and, later, work to improve their writing. If you teach in a workshop in which a form of musical expression other than hip-hop predominates, use that form to open doors for poetic expression as well.

Let's turn to K-Swift's conception of hip-hop; he taught us much about where to start researching the history of hip-hop in the first place.

**Student Profile: K-Swift**

My full name is Anthony Maurice Scott Junior. I was born on September 27th, 1981. I've been rapping since I was 3 years old, and I continue to write and live on the Lower East Side of Manhattan, across the street from "Alphabet City," in Baruch Houses. Most of my writing draws upon what I see in the neighborhood. My favorite time of the year is summer—it's the season when everyone is outside during the evenings. I come home from work and find a place to sit, observe, and laugh with friends. It's very relaxing.

I'm a Senior at Poly Prep Country Day School in Bay Ridge, Brooklyn. Alongside rapping, I wrestle as well. Last year, I was both Ivy League and New York State Private School Wrestling Champion at 121 pounds. This year, I hope to reclaim those titles, and place top 8 at the National Prep School Tournament, qualifying me as an All-American. Next year, I hope to attend NYU, Vassar, UPenn, or Wesleyan.

Though I've lived in many places over the course of my life, from Hawaii to Tennessee, Kentucky to New York City, Brownsville, Brooklyn will always be "home" to me. Whenever we moved from one place to the other, we always stopped in Brownsville, where my Grandmother lives, and my mother grew up. It's a very tough neighborhood, much tougher than the

Lower East Side in Manhattan, and I guess you could say a lot of my writing draws on what I saw and experienced there.

To me, hip-hop is simply a form of urban youth expression. However, the art cultivated by urban youth has expanded across the country into rural and suburban areas, and into the hands of older people, too. I feel that the best rap is rap with a moral, a lesson, a sense of the positive. Unfortunately, it seems like a large portion of the hip-hop culture has been tainted by a lust for money. Many rappers rap about absolutely nothing. Those who express the "violence they see" don't take it anywhere. I like to take the conditions of the ghetto, where life is always harder, and somewhat valueless in the eyes of mainstream society. I try to distill the positivity within it.

Coming from where we come from, my family and friends identify better with hip-hop than poetry. It's probably not surprising that my friends see me as more of an emcee than a poet. I've considered myself an emcee for about 6 years. As far as my rap influences go, my favorite emcees of all time are Rakim and Tupac—Rakim because he was so far ahead of other rappers of his time, rhyming polysyllabically, when most rappers were still struggling with two syllables. Tupac touched my heart with his raw storytelling ability, through describing what he felt about being black in America.

My uncle (only 4 years my senior) and my mother are two of my greatest influences as an emcee. When I was 12, he and I both rapped together. We started out with violent rhymes that lacked a message, but later, due to criticism from my mother (his sister), we changed, and began to write more heart-felt, truer rhymes. She asked us why we were writing the raps that I now consider trash—and I think that turned my writing around completely.

I have always felt that rap was poetry, but I didn't feel that what I wrote were "poems." I was immersed in rap music from birth. I feel that poetry is harder to write, because it is less restricted by rhythm and tone. It is also not the work that I grew up with. But Maureen Weiss' way of teaching had a big impact on me as a writer [Maureen was K-Swift's first teacher at Youth Speaks]. In fact, she was the first person who ever called me a "writer." This was at our last work-shop together.

Can we open ourselves to using this complex and significant cultural form in an environment that is challenging and empowering? Can we teach writing to teenagers on the basis of their own poetic expertise by fostering their development in a social and poetic project of their own choosing? In *Black Music* (1968), LeRoi Jones (also known as Amiri Baraka) criticizes any merely aesthetic understanding of jazz:

> The major flaw in this approach . . . is that it strips the music too ingenuously of its social and cultural intent. It seeks to define jazz as an art (or a folk art) that has come out of no intelligent body of socio-critical philosophy. (14)

Can we avoid a similar problem when we analyze hip-hop and the students who are inspired by it?

Our work with K-Swift offers a vital example of how you can foster such creative work in your own classroom.

You may worry that you don't know much about hip-hop. Does that lack of knowledge pose an obstacle to working with hip-hop in the workshop process? We don't think so; rather, we think it is a boon because when you encounter unfamiliar terrain, you must listen instead of seeking refuge in what you already know.

What you need is not expertise in this culture, but an open mind and the ability to pick out significant aspects of this extremely rhythmic and musical method of writing—and the willingness to ask for *more* of what works in students' poems.

Though teachers who welcome hip-hop as a poetic technique should prepare to hear serious descriptions of life in a society riddled with serious problems, we will hear about everyday teen life, as well: The poems of a given day's workshop will range from the problems of gentrification to the tumble and rush of romantic love to the unappetizing sight of a dead pigeon (as one poet glibly wrote in her piece "Pigeon Filet"). Let's face it: Teen poetry workshops must be a place to have some *fun*. And for teachers, having fun is only possible when we have carved a pedagogical space that lets us be surprised. That space depends on our being attuned to the aspects of hip-hop that can be used to teach our students effective and oftentimes explosive writing skills. To do this, we should understand at least two of the core features of hip-hop, elements that can be readily located in its family tree, which is not the canon of English poetry, but jazz and the blues.

In his *Blues People*, Jones notes two prominent features of the blues and its musical sources: *polyphonic rhythm* and *significant tone* (or *timbre*). Although the central role of these features may seem obvious to us today, they were either unrecognized or wholly ignored by Western listeners who first encountered them in the blues. Those listeners failed to appreciate the deep complexity of the blues, because they analyzed it in terms of their previous musical experience, according to the harmonic and melodic styles of Western classical music. They not only misunderstood *why* the blues did what it did at the level of harmony (diminishing certain notes in otherwise familiar Western scales), they misunderstood the blues at its most *fundamental, structural level* as well. The consequences of that misunderstanding were dire for Western listeners' initial analysis and evaluation of the blues as an aesthetic and social form.

As teachers, we must be careful first to not fail to notice rhythmic complexity in our students' work (especially when it is informed by hip-hop), and second to pay attention to how our students react as an audience to the reading of hip-hop influenced poetry. Simply put, if we know that our students value rhythm above other poetic devices, we should find poems that offer rhythmic complexity, and cheer on the refinement of rhythm in their writing even as we strive to improve the content of the writing itself.

Good teachers find ways to influence their students by marking what the students are doing well, then offering sources that can supplement a student's particular strengths and pique her interest in reading, looking, or listening more widely. Spoken-word writers not only love to write in syncopated verse, they love to read and perform others' syncopated verse as well. If we offer only rhythmically predictable verse, we may fail to take advantage of the tremendous opportunity that hip-hop's popular and influential voice affords us to encourage our students' desire to complicate the way they write, which is first and foremost writing for performance.

Here is an exercise for playing with rhythm: Read two Gerard Manley Hopkins poems, "Pied Beauty" and "God's Grandeur," out loud in a straight, nondynamic tone, asking the class to not pay attention to words they don't understand, just to listen to the rhythms. Now ask your rappers to read the poems as hip-hop lyrics. Reading them this way brings the poems to life. Now ask the class how they think these poems work. Draw connections to writers in the workshop who are using similar devices in their own writing. Finally, ask what benefits and drawbacks there are in connecting poetic forms across different personal identities.

When the first Western listeners compared the Afro-centered blues to the canon of Western music tradition, they saw only what the blues was lacking in comparison to Western music. They ignored what was most complicated, enjoyable, and fundamental to this music—rhythmic texture and tonal shifts. That is precisely what teachers do when they consider spoken word and hip-hop solely as *writing* (or simply analyze how it looks on the page), rather than regarding it as a complex of written, visual, and aural performances.

This critical failure made listeners unable to understand the role of significant tone in the improvisational, oral context of the blues. By privileging written scores over a repetitious structure built for oral improvisation, Western listeners could not appreciate the deep function of tonal changes as bearers of new meanings in repeated lyrics. As Jones notes,

> The meaning of a word can be changed simply by altering the *pitch* of the word, or changing its stress— basically, the way one can change the word *yeh* from simple response to stern challenge simply by moving the tongue slightly. (26)

In an improvisational context, the value of a song or a poem can be determined as much by its rhythmic structure as it is by the flexibility the lyrical form offers for changing meaning through variances in tone, often with no change in the lyrics. We concentrate only on the words our students write, rather than on the inflections that lend new meaning to the words they perform, we will miss the point of spoken-word poetry as an oral, visual, and aural experience.

When K-Swift began attending Youth Speaks workshops, we were struck by the sheer rhythmic and tonal sophistication of his poems. In this chapter, we take a detailed look at one of the poems he brought to our attention, "Mean Streets," to show how teachers can find depth in hip-hop poetry and begin to find places for improvement and growth.

## Mean Streets
### Anthony "K-Swift" Scott

I live by the mean streets                                        1
where many cold hearted teens meet
I'm tryin' to live my life in a clean sweep
I need sleep
but dreams can't be reached in the hood            5
kids'll rather run up in the spot and reach for
    the wood
Or rather the steel
they're hustlin' to grab a meal
they bust shots, hop trains, stab and steal
They buck cops, pop chains, slash and kill        10
at bus stops, not planes, that's the deal
They only know quick money, no longevity
ain't got the ability to be strong and heavenly
Equipped with the wrong weaponry
with minds crippled like victims of leprosy       15
Thugs step to me
we all deal with these ghetto issues
I'm tired of seein' my brothers dyin' behind metal
    missiles
Take my words in and let 'em hit you
life isn't a game, we have to get official        20
Changes must be made
no more death over dough
no more innocent children bein' left on the flo
No more gangs with beef
I hope the thugs don't become angered with me     25
'cause I'm scared of living dangerously
I can't go to another funeral
                              due to a murder
committed by the regular crime with the usual
    burner
You ain't gotta stay in slums you can move further  30

But we gotta rise
to save a lotta lives
since everybody dies

When we read "Mean Streets" as it is formatted here, we need to be aware of some crucial features in the way K-Swift writes. The line breaks show where he breathes or pauses in his delivery. K-Swift doesn't subordinate the reading of his rhymes to the "look" of the line; instead, he creates lines to mirror his breathing pattern, effectively determining their length by the measure or rhythm of his vocal or musical sensibility. Though this method is rigid in terms of tempo and rhythm, it gives a fluidity to the way K-Swift's lines break on paper, and explains why the lines do not syllabically match up in the way teachers might expect from an unforced end-rhymed poem. Simply put, K-Swift doesn't struggle to fit his lines into a consistent visual length or an essentially syllabic structure—he constructs lines primarily by vocalized stresses. When asked how he developed this intricate method of rhyming, K-Swift commented:

> Rap is pure rhythm. You have the beat and you rap to the beat. You go over it and you have to keep a rhyme scheme. I usually hum a rhythm, and that becomes a rhyme scheme. I like to be as innovative as possible. I try to rhyme more and more syllables at a time. I try to rhyme entire sentences, all the while making sense.

Given the tumbling, interlocking movement "Mean Streets" achieves, along with K-Swift's original audience for it (the hip-hop community), we need to examine the poem's effects as part of a sweeping performative gesture, a vocal rolling of images and phrased sentences lodged between long pauses—not simply in terms of single, isolated lines on a page. K-Swift often reads lines in clusters of three or four before he takes an extended, dramatic break. The effect is one of bombardment, in which he forefronts a deep understanding of *alliteration* and *alliterative effect* (the repetition of certain consonants in stressed and unstressed sounds, respectively)—two terms we explain in the analysis of the poem that follows.

Given his preoccupation with the aesthetic devices of his writing, does K-Swift consider his poem's content to be significant? When we asked why he wrote "Mean Streets" in the way he did, he moved from thinking in terms of poetic device to the issue of content:

> "Mean Streets" is one of my favorite pieces, because it functions well as both a rap piece and a poem. I wrote it as an expression of the violence I've seen, and I've known others to go through. This is my personal experience and the experience of others, translated into a piece with a moral. I see this work as a social commentary: I want my poetry to teach, not simply tell a pointless story.

When K-Swift's teacher, Maureen Weiss, first heard this poem, she felt that its rhythmic and tonal directness worked in tandem with its sharp report to create a message of bleakness, and yet of unmistakable hope. The distinct, monosyllabic *end rhymes* in the first eleven lines created "a constant impression of typewriter keys, sounding like the gunshots described in his poem." This offers us an excellent starting place to analyze and teach "Mean Streets" within the workshop. When we study a student's work, we begin with the most salient features, then later strive to foster the group's discovery of the poem's hidden subtleties, thereby helping the workshop members to understand the poem at progressively deeper levels.

For simplicity, we focus here on the poem's first eleven lines. In a workshop, we would have a student transcribe this short section onto an easel pad or dry-erase board while K-Swift read the poem aloud. We would use different colored pens to denote the different aspects of the poem noticed by the students. Here we use boldface, italics, and underlining to perform the same function.

K-Swift's overlay of short words and staccato beats creates the sound of typewriter keys and gunshots, as it melds the dangers of the street into a recognizable rhythmic frame. This effect is created by the poem's persistent use of *end rhymes* drawing from a long stressed "e" sound. Of the eleven lines presented here, only one, line 10, varies that use, by rhyming line 9's "steal" with "kill." This is an example of *slant rhyme* (a rhyme in which one of the sounds is slightly modified), and offers a fine opportunity to address the workshop on the subtle possibility of using modified rhymes within a consistent rhythmic scheme. Here are the first eleven lines, with end-rhymed words in boldface:

<blockquote>

I live by the mean **streets**                    1
where many cold hearted teens **meet**
I'm tryin' to live my life in a clean **sweep**
I need **sleep**
but dreams can't be reached in the **hood**        5
kids'll rather run up in the spot and reach for the
   **wood**
Or rather the **steel**
they're hustlin' to grab a **meal**
they bust shots, hop trains, stab and **steal**
They buck cops, pop chains, slash and **kill**      10
at bus stops, not planes, that's the **deal**

</blockquote>

We immediately become aware of something else in the poem— a subtle use of *internal rhyme* (rhyme within a single line). Here are the lines with the internal rhymes set in boldface italic:

<blockquote>

I live by the ***mean* streets**                  1
where many cold hearted ***teens* meet**
I'm tryin' to live my life in a ***clean* sweep**
I need **sleep**
but ***dreams*** can't be ***reached*** in the **hood**   5
kids'll rather run up in the spot and ***reach*** for the
   **wood**
Or rather the **steel**

</blockquote>

they're hustlin' to *grab* a **meal**
they bust *shots, hop trains, stab* and **steal**
They buck *cops, pop chains*, slash and **kill**　　　　10
at bus *stops, not planes*, that's the **deal**

What does drawing our attention to both end rhymes and internal rhymes achieve? It helps us concentrate on the way K-Swift reads the poem. By asking K-Swift to reread the first two lines, we can show what his internal rhyme allows—a decisive stress on "*streets*" in the first line and a stress on the second-to-last word in the next line. In reading it as "*teens* meet," K-Swift end-rhymes off of *teen*, creating a dangling effect, a dispersal, and a drawing away from the simple rhyme scheme we might expect.

Such deceptive complexity returns us to Maureen's reflections on first hearing the poem, which she described as "sounding like a new language, making the piece take on a beat I had never heard before." Clearly, Maureen was speaking of something other than K-Swift's end rhymes. We ask the students, What is K-Swift doing in addition to the end rhyme? That question is a variation of one that's central to how we appreciate each poet in our workshop: What exactly in this poet's language feels new? In K-Swift's case, the answer is not long in coming—the rolling feel of his lines (the movement from stressed to unstressed sounds), as well as the use of rhymes that precede and even follow his end rhymes, offers us something special to teach: K-Swift is doing a fine job of flustering the ear's propensity to predict repetition by drawing his audience's attention away from the end rhymes that undergird the poem.

With an eye on the rolling stresses of the lines, here are all the other rhymes that complicate K-Swift's performance of the poem. Newly recognized rhymes are italicized here:

*I* live *by* the **mean streets**　　　　　　　　　　1
where *many* cold hearted **teens meet**
*I*'m *tryin'* to live *my life* in a **clean sweep**
*I* need *sleep*
but **dreams** can't be **reached** *in the hood*　　　　5

kids'll *rather* run up in the spot and **reach** *for the*
   *wood*
Or *rather the* **steel**
they're hustlin' to *grab a* **meal**
they ***bust shots, hop trains, stab and* steel**
They ***buck cops, pop chains, slash and* kill**          10
at ***bus stops, not planes, that's the* deal**

We draw the class to notice the range of K-Swift's style in action by asking members to underline key features of the poem in different colors of ink. K-Swift is not simply rhyming on the end of the line; he is rhyming at the front of the line as well. At lines 5 and 6, he rhymes *after* the end rhyme, juxtaposing "in the hood" with "for the wood," and refreshes the dangling effect. Finally, in the last four lines of this section, K-Swift rhymes three entire phrases with each other—not only *within* the lines, but *between* the lines, too. This dense phrasal rhyming creates the effect of a polysyllabic rhyme in a single word. And once we pay attention to the rhymed phrases, to the rhymed complex he is employing, we recognize that K-Swift is also rhyming phrases in lines 1 and 3, 4 and 5, and 7 and 8.

In this stunning display, K-Swift works with *consonance* (piling repetition of consonants) and *assonance* (repetition of vowels). Noting how he uses these devices gives us a sense that he already understands the basis of *sprung rhythm* (defined both as a counting of *stressed sounds* instead of syllables, and as a sudden creation of rhythm inside a line effected by consonance and assonance). To forefront these devices, we draw the workshop's attention to the section's final four lines, using underlines beneath the letter responsible for the effect. Pay particular attention not only to the rhyming phrases, but also to K-Swift's repetition of the consonants *l, m, n, r,* and *s,* and the vowel sounds *ah* and *uh.*

they're *hustlin'* to *grab a meal*          8
they *bust* shots, *hop* trains, st*ab and* steel          9
They *buck* c*ops, pop* chains, sl*ash and* kill          10
at *bus* st*ops, not* planes, th*at's the* deal          11

The rhymes in this section stack up on an eight-syllable line, with K-Swift deftly mixing all the devices we have noted, from end rhyme to a complex pattern of polysyllabic rhyming and alliteration, thereby creating a flurry of sounded "pops" not unlike the rolling of a drum between sections of a jazz song—or gunfire.

Direct the class to notice how K-Swift orients his audience—it is significant that his poem was meant to be performed as a rap before it was meant to be read as a poem. Ask the students to look for key repetitions that have nothing to do with rhyme or alliterative effect. If we look for such evidence, we soon see that K-Swift grounds his poem on a solid narrative scene, using "I" and "they" six times in the section's eleven lines. What does noting this buried poetic feature do for the discussion? It shows that even while K-Swift's poem provides the workshop with a vital example of how rhythm can be used to render an extremely restricted complex of rhymes unpredictable—"Mean Streets" highlights the necessary task of orienting one's listeners, maintaining narrative stability as the poem's rhythmic and tonal qualities grow increasingly more complicated.

Once we recognized what K-Swift's poetry could offer a workshop, we decided to craft an entire class around the topic of rhythm. We constructed an exercise, planned for students to write and perform it, and arranged for a visit from a renowned spoken-word poet we had studied throughout the workshop—Tracie Morris, the author of two books of poetry (*Intermission* and *Chap-T-Her Won*) and a former Nuyorican Grand Slam Champion.

We asked Tracie to read a poem that we had listened to earlier in the workshop, "Gangsta Suite." This striking poem's opening lines read

I. Who Knew?

Thought I had my shit together
I was feeling fly whatever
Feather hanging with the chickies looking dope.
Hoping I was doing better snapping on them foolish
    fellas
looking too hard scoping this cutie, I was like, 'nope.'

As Tracie read in her characteristically quick tempo, she spontaneously improvised and repeated select phrases, replicating the jarring stutter-step effect of hip-hop deejays spinning turntables. Tracie's spontaneous delivery was electric, and it seemed to heighten the workshop member's sense that the performance of a poem takes priority over its written form.

But after she finished reading, a curious thing happened: Tracie explained that in the spoken-word scene, there is a fundamental difference between poets who are essentially *actors* and those who are *poets* in the strict sense. The actor is the writer who exaggerates the importance of delivery over that of the written word. The poet is the writer who crafts her work so that it can remain on the page and still convey meaning. The poem "answers for itself."

This distinction spurred a discussion that ultimately hinged on the question of how hip-hop is different from poetry. Here is what K-Swift had to say:

> Rap is pure rhythm—you have the beat and you rap to the beat. You go over it and you have to keep a rhyme scheme. Poetry is more free. It's harder for me to write, I guess. A poem can have a beat underneath it, but it's not direct because you have the freedom to stray from the rhythm and then come back to it or you can stick with it all along. In poetry you can be a lot more figurative and abstract and with rap you can't do that. You have to be concrete . . .

What did bringing Tracie Morris into the workshop do for K-Swift, given that he feels such a gulf exists between rap and poetry, and given that she combines the forms so eloquently? K-Swift explained that he was struck by Tracie's combination of jazz scat, rap, and traditionally poetic styles, which presented him with creative possibilities for integrating all three styles into his own work. "She sort of found a middle ground," he commented later. "She gave me ideas, in terms of performing, how I could change up my style."

An even more significant encounter between K-Swift and Tracie occurred later in the workshop when we performed an exercise with K-Swift's poem (Exercise 9 in the next section). We asked him to write the first ten lines of his poem on the easel pad, then read it aloud, and we alerted the workshop members to pay attention to where he emphasized tone and rhythm. After this, one student marked the places where K-Swift had paused, stressed sounds, or gestured for performative effect. We then gave Tracie a red pen and asked her and the group to suggest places where K-Swift could pause or stress sounds that he had not stressed in his first reading. Our goal was to radically change the way K-Swift read his poem, to move him away from the beat he had so assiduously worked to define. And when K-Swift read this new version, the workshop agreed that something had happened to the original rap they'd heard only five minutes before. Keeping their distinction between rap and poetry in mind, the students did not feel they were listening to a more intricate *rap*—instead, they adamantly held that they were listening to something else entirely, a *poem*. (It is essential to note that there was no approbation attached to the term *poem*. The students held only that the two readings were merely different, with the latter seeming more "poetic.") We asked K-Swift how this exercise affected his writing, and he had this to say:

> When she worked with my rap, I felt somewhat threatened. She questioned my rhythm. When I rap, I keep one solid tempo, but she wanted me to translate the words into a new rhythm. I felt that this strategy would be valuable for other works, but not this specific piece.

Does the fact that K-Swift felt threatened, or that it was essentially unhelpful to rewriting "Mean Streets," mean the exercise failed? Though K-Swift was reluctant to celebrate the exercise outright, it *did* ignite his thinking about the possibilities of writing poetry, and began to change the way he approached later poems and raps.

As teachers, we know that teen writers often feel threatened when we first ask them to experiment. But we hope that the first three weeks of a spoken-word poetry workshop will lead students to a genuine commitment to experimenting in the poems they will write. That is exactly what happened with K-Swift.

We must also consider the effect that working with K-Swift's poem had on the workshop group as a whole. Watching one of their most talented poets experiment with precisely the thing that he is most gifted in achieving—rhythm and tone—was of tremendous instructive value.

By the third week of the workshop, you should feel comfortable bringing some of your best writers' work before the class for deep reading. Not only will the class see why certain aspects of the writing work well, they will also see that even the workshop's most accomplished writers have plenty of room for improvement.

## Nine Exercises in Rhythm and Tone for Week Three

The true test of these exercises is in how the sounds are produced, and their real success derives from the diversity of rhythms and tones that the group expresses, so the exercises should be read aloud by as many of the writers in the workshop as possible.

*1. Take 5.* Each person writes a four-line rhymed stanza based on the same theme (from love to violence to hope), using their own natural rhyme scheme. The writers then pass their work to the left and continue writing by working off the stanza now before them. Have five rounds of writing, then read these collective poems aloud and discuss what working in other people's rhythms was like. Also talk about which of the group's poems are satisfying as a whole, and why.

*2. Terza Rima.* Students construct a series of three-line stanzas with a syllable count of their choosing, using *terza rima* (end rhymes have the sequence *aba bcb cdc ded*). Discuss whether the rhyme scheme or the syllable count confined or liberated their voices (consider K-Swift's feeling that it is easier to write within metric guidelines). Ask how using a set rhyme scheme affects the poem's line-by-line content as well as its meaning.

*3. Changing Stations on the Radio.* Break the workshop into groups of three and give all the groups the same poem to perform—*as a musical group*, with each using a different kind of music: bebop jazz, hip-hop/rap, slow country-Western, Bob Dylan, or Ani DiFranco style folk, heavy metal. Within each group, one student taps or snaps (or beat boxes) the drum beat, one hums the bass line, and one performs the vocals by either reading or singing the poem. Gwendolyn Brooks' poem "We Real Cool" is good for this exercise, but any poem with a rhyme scheme will work. Ask how the rhythm affects the mood of the poem, and how the influence of a diversity of sounds can lead to performative advantages.

*4. Writing to a Differently Bouncing Ball.* Play a popular hip-hop tune and have the students write over the beat while they listen. Read their work aloud. Repeat using a bebop or Charles Mingus jazz tune. Repeat with a reggae song. When the music stops, ask a volunteer to read one stanza aloud while the rest of the group tries to reconstruct the beat over which the poem was written and guesses what musical selection it came from. Finally, have students pair off and work together to join all three sections into one poem, arranging them in any order. Have them read these aloud, then discuss how rhythmic variety can add to the overall complexity of poetry.

*5. When Writing in Rome.* Have the students write short poems with an unfamiliar (or nonidiomatic) syllabic formation, such as a haiku (three lines, five-seven-five) or a Tanka (five lines, varying). Ask them to rigidly adhere to the form, even if it means considering creative options such as chopping a polysyllabic word in half, bringing a word to the next line, or shortening a word as it is pronounced, as in "flo" for "floor." Discuss what kinds of performative consequences extreme rhythmic constraints can create.

6. *Don't Judge a Poem by Its Cover.* Bring in a poem and ask one student to read it aloud as she sees it on the page. Then have another person read it in a radically different way, exaggerating line breaks (enjambment or its opposite) or vocally stressing certain inconspicuous words over other, more salient ones. Ask a third reader to quicken or slow down the second reader's pace. Discuss how these different readings changed the poem's tone and meaning. Then, discuss how certain kinds of readings can be conveyed by marks on the page, using techniques like *enjambment*—ending a line in the middle of a word to produce multiple meanings. A good poem for this exercise is June Jordan's "Roman Poem Number Fourteen" from her book *Haruko/Love Poems* (1993).

7. *The Difference Between Slam and Psalm Is One Letter.* Videotape a televangelist and have the students watch at least a five-minute section, writing down everything they notice about his tone, hand gestures, and body language. Stop the tape and ask the students to consider how the speaker's tone and performance enhance or hinder his message. Have the students write short poems using the televangelist's tone. The content may or may not have anything to do with familiar televangelical content. Consider how using the tone of televangelical worship to perform secular content can create surprising irony, with very little or no change in the way the poem is written.

8. *Welcome to the Jingle.* Videotape three advertisements on daytime local television: a nostalgic commercial, a car dealership offering "fantastic" deals, and a restaurant describing its food in the language of succor. Have students mark the tonal qualities of each, then write poems on any topic but using the tone and rhythm of their favorite ad. Ask how writing in that tone or rhythm determined the content of what they wrote.

**9. *Marking Rhythm for New Meaning.*** Take the first eight lines of one of your student's poems and write them on an easel pad. Have the student read her poem aloud, asking someone to underline which words she stresses as she reads. Next, have the group arbitrarily pick words to stress and add wide pauses in places where the author would never add a line break. Have the student reread her poem according to these changes, then ask the group how the meaning of the poem has changed. Consider how the student feels about reworking her poem in this way, and whether or not the class likes the second version better.

# week ■■■ 4 ■ The Politics of Poetry

*I noticed her leg kept on beating as she read one of her poems,
a reflex you only see on people who are deeply involved and
genuinely into what they're doing. Most people couldn't see her
leg and I'm sure she didn't even realize she was moving it. It
was one of those instinctive movements or maybe she did it
intentionally to help her develop and keep up with the rhythm
of the poem. It was the smallest detail that caught my eye and
engraved itself in my memory. As petty as her moving her leg
to the beat of the poem may sound, it's what showed me how
involved and how passionate she really is in and about the art
form, and how sincere she was about everything she said.*

—Charles Wekselbaum, 17 (on seeing poet Sonia Sanchez)

*To write as if your life depended on it: to write
across the chalkboard, putting up there in public words
you have dredged, sieved up from dreams, from behind
screen memories, out of silence—words you have dreaded
and needed in order to know you exist.*

—Adrienne Rich (1993, 33)

In the fourth week of a Youth Speaks workshop, we want to expand
our students' sense of what the terms *politics* and *political* mean.
With a week of conversations about the central role of politics in the
development of spoken-word poetry (and a bit about politics in
general), we aim to help our writers understand how political
issues—issues of power and people's perspective on and relation-

76

ship to it—can function in their poetry—how they can sharpen their poems by developing and expressing their political voices.

To expose the students to the rich history of politics in spoken-word poetry, watch one or two documentaries on the civil rights movement and its development into the social movements of the 1970s. (*Memphis to Montgomery* and *Eyes on the Prize* are fine documentaries to screen.) It makes sense to watch these films at this stage in the workshop because the students have written and performed for three weeks and should be ready to appreciate the range of social issues they can include in their work. Watching these films gives young writers a broader sense not only of what they can accomplish as poets, but also of what kinds of political and social claims their poems can make. The fourth week is also a fruitful time to discuss the history of spoken-word poetry: After three weeks, the students should be ready to learn about the art movement underlying what may have seemed like unconnected assignments.

Why set aside an entire week to discuss politics? The answer lies in understanding the most influential expansion of the spoken-word movement, which stemmed from the work of the Nuyorican Poets during the 1980s and '90s. During this time, spoken word evolved into a national phenomenon, culminating in the beginnings of the National Poetry Slam. Perhaps the most important reasons for this expansion were spoken word's new, relaxed manner of presenting poetry; its celebration of multiculturalism; and its deep commitment to expressing the issues faced by traditionally marginalized (and silenced) social groups. (We believe that teenagers constitute a marginalized social group in any era.)

The value of knowing these things about spoken word is immense, because when you know them, you know that your class doesn't merely reflect your teacherly ideas of open-minded literature, but is also part of an art movement. The notion that important and complicated art could be enjoyed by people from all backgrounds required a good deal of fighting to be accepted: It is in this sense that spoken word immediately and forever came to be considered "political" poetry.

Spoken-word poetry was founded on an acceptance of all cultures, social types, and voices. As an art movement, it continues to value diversity and inclusion above other features. We should make this clear in a tacit way throughout the workshop, but in the fourth week, we should be explicit about how diversity and acceptance are central to this art movement as a whole and why forefronting those two qualities in the 1980s and '90s was a political act through and through.

The following paragraphs briefly describe the politics of the poetry of this period, a period that proved central to the current flowering of the movement. Ultimately, we think the following description can explain why the term *spoken-word poetry* is almost always associated with politically charged writing. Thus, though we expect the individual issues of this kind of poetry to continue to change as we write, we believe its basic themes and overall sensibility will remain quite stable.

A workshop teacher doesn't need to be an expert on the history of spoken-word poetry, but he does need to have a sense of spoken word's traditional openness to different perspectives so he can ask workshop students to have the same kind of openness.

## A Brief Characterization of Spoken Word

If one commonality binds spoken-word poets together, it is that when they perform, their poems are always urgent and necessary enough to compel the audience to listen carefully. The language and content of their performed work tends to be less concerned with the dense phrasings and abstractions of "readerly" poetry (such as the work of Wallace Stevens or William Butler Yeats, which requires two or three readings to make much sense at all) than with establishing a vital, visceral communication with the audience. These poets collect their urgent language from the streets, from phrases whispered between friends, from their households, from the language of lovers—from all the languages people use to convey our thoughts with immediacy. The urgency of the language suggests that the poet is speaking words from the heart, improvising without troubling over how the words come out.

It is this combination of improvisation, urgency, and the familiarity of our common language that makes spoken word arresting. The spoken-word poet is a poet in the fullest sense of the word—his language, though it may be structured by the grammar of the everyday, is chiseled, rhythmic, and finely detailed. Only a true poet can respond to the rigid—and often critically unrecognized—demands of speaking urgent feelings and ideas in everyday, accessible language by creating poetry that leaps from the mouth with power and wit.

At its most effective, spoken word is poetry through and through, a poetry that can be accessed by anyone who speaks the language, felt by anyone who can relate to the poet's writing and performance. A hybrid of the streets and the abstract domain of poetry, performed before crowds that shout with knowing joy at a well-crafted phrase, spoken word in part depends on its resonance with the way we speak because its poetry exists in the subtle ways the poet bends, shapes, and polishes everyday language into a crystalline, refined, and sublimated version of itself—into a poetry of its own.

Because of its hybrid nature, spoken-word poetry has always been a political form; indeed, its origins suggest that it rebelled against the interests, power, and domination of what could be called academic poetry. This version of the poetry reading typically featured an established adult poet reading to a primarily white, university-educated audience. The spoken-word movement sought from the beginning to leave behind the high brow definition of what real poetry was. Spoken-word poetry was thus political partly because it called itself poetry without the affirmation of the American poetic institution. The poems were not written for the enjoyment of the academy, but for the people who came to see and cheer for the new poets and their real American voices—young people and adults who spoke from their own languages and experiences and wrote to express the urgent issues that their audiences were facing.

Spoken word isn't the only kind of poetry that has used the vernacular to achieve a political purpose. Indeed, the roots of spoken-word poetry go far deeper than this simple description might suggest. Spoken word developed from many strands of writing, from the oracular traditions of the blues, the Beats, and, of course, rap, to name only the most salient influences. All of these strands have an undeniable commonality: a community of writers who wished to express themselves outside of the conventional frame of "serious" poetry. Of course, the boundaries between spoken word and "serious" poetry are blurry and dubious, anyway—there really are no fixed differences between a Browning dramatic monologue and a well-crafted poem from the point of view of a mother who has lost her children to drugs and abuse—but in the flowering of the spoken-word movement, many established writers and critics were initially reluctant to champion the movement because the poetry wasn't "serious" or "complicated" enough to warrant serious consideration. (This in spite of the fact that few of these writers found themselves waging the same complaint against Browning.)

The reasons for this have as much to do with class, race, sexuality, and politics as anything else. Because it concentrated on the politics and poetics of the oppressed, spoken word was not originally blessed with the esteem of the academy. Only now, after the academic attitude toward art has shifted and hip-hop has earned both mainstream and critical appreciation, has spoken-word poetry begun to be recognized as a rich and viable aesthetic form. It has always championed the voices of writers, adults and teenagers alike, who have felt the effects of marginalization.

One such writer in the Youth Speaks program is Alex Fishman, whose poetry speaks for itself through a sharp sense of detail, surprising thematic content, and sparseness of line. Here is Alex's poem "Just to Keep Warm":

## Just to Keep Warm
**Alex Fishman**

On the way to school
I asked Jon about chimneys
Why do we need them?

He told me it's so other people can know
when we are warm in front of a fire,
and when the fire is out and we sit in the dark

shirtless, his hands around me
holding me close, so tight
our fingers leave marks

Read this poem out loud to your workshop and discuss the way Alex uses perspective to generate mood, rhythm, and specificity. Here are some questions that can lead to vital discussions not only about Alex's poem, but about the work of any student in the workshop.

- Is the language of this poem effective, given the subject matter? Do language and subject work together? Does one need to be improved before the other? How?
- Who is the author writing for, and how do you think this audience will react?
- Who feels the author is writing for *them*—that the author is speaking of experiences they too have shared?
- Could this poem be turned into a rallying cry? Would it gain or lose power as a result?

It is our job as workshop teachers to provide a platform for all our developing student writers, marginalized or not, and to help them improve their poetry detail by detail. This process starts in the fourth week by breaking down the way students think of the term *political* in their writing.

Your workshop can model itself on the professional spoken-word audience, which recognizes diversity and inclusion as its very essence, by nurturing all of the students' voices with equal respect. You can achieve this throughout the workshop by thinking in terms of "finding our commonality through our unique experiences."

## Changing the Way Students Think of the Term Political

In the third week of the workshop, we temporarily redefined the way our class understood *meaning* in order to foster an environment based on listening and positive feedback. In the fourth week we want to redefine *political*. Most students respond to the word as though it connotes only the trappings of government, but the term can be extended from government to issues of class, race, and gender—all the way down the line.

To consider the word in its widest possible sense, we should define it as implying an *entrenched perspective*, a perspective that hinges on a person or social group's experience of power or prestige, weakness or alienation. When we consider the term *politics* in this sense, we can see why spoken-word poems would be so successful in generating audience response. For when a poet speaks from his experiences and makes judgments based on those experiences, we, as the audience, are likely to find ourselves on one side or the other. Depending on the way the poet chooses to play with our reaction, the effect can be as electric as the poet's imagination.

The workshop's goal should be to improve the details, rhythm, and politics of genuinely perspectival self-expression—however that expression manifests itself. This fourth week, we are far less interested in getting our students to write poems about presidential politics, tax distribution, or drilling in the Arctic Circle (though any of these topics could wind up in an effective poem) than in getting them to express their own perspectives on their social experiences. When a student's experiences are verbalized before the group, they in effect become political expressions. Since teenagers share so many of the same experiences and are subject to the power and powerlessness of so many forces, the effect of a poem written from the heart is often electric to the workshop as a whole.

A story from one of our Youth Speaks workshops offers a fine example of this idea in action. In a recent class, one of our students wrote a poem about a man disrespecting a woman. Initially, she was embarrassed at the way her poem was written. She had no idea how much she moved the class, which immediately responded to the issue at an emotional level. Many of the women and men in the class came forward with stories of similar experiences in their own relationships, and thanked the poet for her honesty. Once this gifted writer recognized that her poem was not only a personal story of her experience (or just an example of awkward phrasing), but a potential rallying cry for the women who would hear it, she realized that it had two roles to play: telling a personal history and reminding the class that there were others in the audience to whom they could speak. Everyone in the class also learned a valuable lesson from experiencing the power of a poet conquering her own fear and striking her audience with honest poetry from the heart. Such moments of sharing are incredible, for they bring an isolated, perhaps solitary writer's experience to an audience and suddenly turn that audience into a community of listeners who not only can relate to the poet's marginalizing experiences, but who likely have shared those experiences as well. Soon the first student's singular, isolated poem had given rise to other inspired poems on the subject of gender and power, among them a group piece that three of our poets performed at the National Poetry Slam in San Francisco. Here is the original, untitled, poem by Michelle J. Cardona:

## Excerpt from "Untitled"
### Michelle J. Cardona

FLICK FLICK
do you even THINK about the neighbor who beats

his wife
her body being thrashed and bashed
like a rag doll's
"You come here" he yells,
"I'm the man of the house!
What I say goes
You do what I TELL you to do
WHAT talking back to me"
beep beep beep beep beeeeeep
her cracked lips uttering their last breath
I remember calling the police but they never came

Last night while trying to put paper to pen
and pen to paper
I couldn't find words to kiss the pages on which I
    wrote
words were teasing me
            hiding and creeping within the limits of my
            mind
I was watching the news but I wasn't listening
What does this mean?
I asked and asked myself
but my remote control finally turned me OFF
CLICK

Teaching the politics of poetry in the fourth week then, need go no
further than helping your students get the sense that the more they
write from their perspectives as members of different kinds of communities—women, teenagers, a certain race or class, and so on—the
more powerful their interaction with their audiences will be.

Of course, not all students are disposed toward writing
politically charged poems. Those of privileged upbringing, gender, or race may even, in an ironic but completely natural way,
feel alienated by their privilege. Teachers must work through this
alienation and strive to draw such writers into the fold: We must
include and accept every voice in the classroom.

If you have students who feel set apart from the others because they have nothing political to say, focus the entire group on thinking about perspective rather than politics. We want students to be confident about writing poems from their experience. That means that a poem about growing up in a mansion with one parent is as important to the workshop as a poem about the dangers of walking home in the crossfire of rival gangs.

Though it may initially seem like a hindrance, dealing with such students is actually a blessing, because part of the beauty of the spoken-word workshop is that it offers a platform for free expression for all students, from all angles, outside of the traditional judgment of the classroom. A student who does not feel political will learn much from students who are writing about racism, being gay, the beauty of a certain poor neighborhood. Whether or not they write political pieces, this week will be a learning experience for everyone in the workshop as they come to know each other in more and more intimate ways.

One of the most amazing poems to come out of this fourth week of writing and thinking in a Youth Speaks workshop was written by Onome Djere, a member of the 2000 New York National Teen Poetry Slam Team. In many ways, Onome's work represents a culmination of the first four weeks of our course, for it combines the spontaneity and surprise of freewriting with the rhythm and politics of the best of today's spoken-word poetry. Here is Onome's poem "Her," followed by her student profile.

## Her

**Onome Djere**

> She always this numb? this quiet? She
> dreams of hellos waved, untainted by cum-
> stained hands
>
> > She ever dream
> of smiles greeting her face without
> the bitter aftertaste of acid eyes lingering on
> her

breasts She always this sullen? Why don't
she
speak up in class she's a black girl
black girls supposed to be loud
She ever cry out loud?
Her tears drip like rain outside a soundproof
window
She ever go to church
catch the holy ghost, receive holy men?
She dance in thongs for thousands a night—
she could work in offices for respectable
pennies,
be called
honey, dear or nothing
She learn to dismiss her anger when he said
he's sick of male bashing poems
He bash her?
She know how many times they said leave
him,
he treats you bad
She know how to feel god?
She ever leave church, become her own?
She always pick at her skin
hiding gold under volcanoes? always
sit cross-legged and silent
hiding gold in her mouth in her womb?
She always eat so little eat so much?
Think too much say little?
Think too much about other's feelings
feel too deeply
fall too deeply in love with wells that held
no water?
She always feel like a streetlight
tryna compete with the moon?

**Student Profile: Onome Djere**

For high school, I went to Whitney Young Magnet in Chicago, where I was born and raised. I'm of Nigerian heritage. I started writing when I was nine. I remember my first desire to write was in 4th grade when my class was assigned to write anti-violence slogans. I remember thinking 80% of them were corny and uninspired, though my reference point for what fresh and passionate looked like wasn't clear.

Intuition later led me to James Baldwin. It was over for me after that. Entered a whole new world.

Youth Speaks provided a space for me to grow as a writer, performer and mentor. One of my highlights from Youth Speaks was being in San Francisco for the 2000 National Teen Slam finals. I did not see that coming at all. That was the first time I had experienced an international community of youth poets. It was such a rush to be among youths who, in the words of Biko (a San Francisco poet), are "scratching the surface of how dope they can be."

I hone my writing to share my view of the world, in all its glory and folly, without being didactic, preachy, or flowery. What I hope to convey is the relentlessness of contradictory messages many young women internalize regarding selfhood in relation to their environment. That brings to mind a line from a Staceyann Chin poem that I feel I've yet to actualize—"I have learnt to pitch/this voice far beyond/the secrets of our silent survival/to reach for the greater intention/to save more than my own life."

Performance-wise, I would say Staceyann Chin, Richard Pryor, John Leguizamo and Dr. Martin Luther

King, Jr. are my main influences. The latter three are not generally thought of as poets, but infusion of words with nuance, passion, honesty, immediacy, conviction and emotional connection is what all four have in common. I can't call Tracie Morris my "favorite" poet, cuz no one else does what she does the way she does it (in terms of sound poetry) to compare her to. Which is to say she's amazing. As for my main literary influences, they are Baldwin, Mike Royko (the famous Chicago editorialist), and Sherman Alexie.

I hope to go to Sarah Lawrence College to concentrate on performance art and writing.

Onome's poem is just one example of what can be generated through the following exercises. In our own workshops, Onome's poetic maturity stood out to all who encountered it. Don't expect that your students will be producing work at the same level of maturity after just a few short weeks. As the rawness of Michelle Cardona's poem illustrates, the beauty of these exercises is their ability to provoke writing that is passionate and personal, and therefore political.

## Exercises for the Fourth Week

*1. Political Worlds, Political Words.* This is an easy exercise to begin the week. Ask everyone to write their ten favorite political words—words that can come from political speeches or anything that resembles politics in their lives. Have everyone swap words, then ask them to use the words they got to write a paragraph-long political speech to convince everyone in the class that something needs to change, now. The goals of these poems should be as big or as small as your student writers make them.

*2. A Passage to Politics.* On your own the night before class, watch *Slam Nation*. Find one poem in the film that you think your students would find suggestive and inspiring. Cue the video to that scene, then bring it into class the next day, and have your workshop watch the passage at least twice. Have the students take notes on what they find interesting from a political point of view: the poet's body language, the poem's themes, the way the poem is delivered, and so on. Go immediately into a writing exercise in which your poets write a "political" poem that reflects (but is not limited to) the things they found interesting while watching the film. Have all the students read their poems. After each, ask the workshop members what specific aspects of the *Slam Nation* poem they think the poet noted and what they themselves think of the new poem. Then have the poet who read explain what he found most interesting in the *Slam Nation* poem and what he was trying to do in his own poem.

*3. Can a Letter Speak for Today's Generation?* Find a tape of Dr. Martin Luther King Jr. reading from his incredible "Letter from a Birmingham Jail" and make photocopies of one of Mumia Abu Jamal's prison writings. Have your workshop listen to King reading, mark the way he delivers his message, and think about how the delivery may be at the heart of what he is saying. After discussing this pathbreaking letter, hand out Mumia Abu Jamal's writing and have one student read it aloud. Ask the students to think about how Mumia may or may not be writing for a specific generation in the same way that King did. Are their concerns significantly similar, or different? How and why? Ask the class members to write a poetic letter from their position in society, drawing upon the strengths they see in the work of these two thinkers.

*4. Is Everything Relative? Exercises on Perspective.* Direct your students to go into a public place between today's class and tomorrow's and notice and describe a captivating person. Ask them to write a three-sentence fictional scene from that character's perspective and in that character's supposed language. Then they will insert another character into the scene, making this character of a different class from the first one and having the new character judge the first one in whatever voice the students imagine the character would have. The next day in class, have the students read their poems aloud. Direct a discussion around the ways people treat each other and how class differences can be (but aren't always) reflected in the way we speak. Talk about how we can use those differences to write and perform poetry to greater effect.

5. *Is Judgment Final?* Direct your writers to describe a time when they were judged and couldn't possibly change the outcome of the judgment. Make it clear that the way they decide to place themselves in their narratives—whether as interested parties with urgent language or as speakers who have digested, dissected, and come to terms with the judgment—will have a massive effect on the poem's dramatic possibilities. (If your poets want to write about how they changed someone's mind, you can also use that to spur effective writing.)

6. *Breathing and the Tone of the Political Message.* In this performance-based exercise, use a videotape of a politician speaking. Have the students analyze the performative aspects of the speech—how the politician breathes, uses his hands, opens his mouth—and anything that's emphatic or repetitive in the delivery. Direct a conversation about the political uses of body movements and how we can draw on them to make (sometimes ironic) statements in our own writing of spoken-word poetry. Have volunteers offer their own performances to the entire workshop and have the class analyze the performances as they did the politician's speech. Break the class into small groups and repeat the exercise to get more intensive feedback.

7. *The Superhero of Your Neighborhood.* This exercise works off of the idea that certain urban myths—myths of local morality, interests, and power—carry with them our deepest feelings about the

way life should be. Direct your students to write about a truly local superhero, one who acts out their hopes and desires.

This exercise asks students to imagine experiences and characters that aren't limited by the usual rules and restrictions that bind them. (For instance, one of our students created a character named Ghetto Man. His superhero was able to rise above the deadly fighting in his neighborhood.) After directing the class to write for ten minutes, ask them to read their work aloud. Discuss the poems, and then move to question the restrictions teens face, and how these characters are answers, if not solutions, to them.

*8. What Flag Do You Follow?* Ask students to meet in groups of five and design a flag that represents their highest values. As two people draw the flag (using graffiti script, hand paint, or whatever medium you like), the other three write a piece in three voices, espousing the values of their new flag. This piece can be as lighthearted or as serious as your students like—even if groups are simply having fun writing a humorous piece, the essential theme of the exercise will come through.

This flag exercise offers an additional way to articulate local politics in an abstract way. After creating these flags, ask the students to think about how diverse values are represented on the flag. Direct the class to think about what values are being celebrated by each flag *before* the creators tell everyone what their flag means. This playful discussion works nicely to prepare the class for the interpretive demands of the final week of revision.

*9. Swapping Gender.* This exercise in narrative is designed to help students think around stubborn problems. Ask them to take a problem they have with the other gender and write a poem about that problem from the other gender's point of view. This new point of view should neither be culpable nor wholly free of guilt—the idea is that looking at the other gender in a new way will let us imagine old problems with a fresh sensibility. This exercise often results in surprising pieces of work.

# ■ ■ ■ 5 ■ Revision and Performance

*I look back now, and realize the words that I missed, the love that I failed to give, cuz I was busy preparing myself. You can only prepare yourself so much. It's not about the 10 and it's certainly not about who will eventually win the Teen Poetry Slam. It may be hard, but try not to lose focus on what your purpose is—to speak to another; to tell someone your story. Words are priceless. You either use them to dance for someone else, or you use them to state yourself.*

—Morgan Cousins, 17

*You cannot write lies and write good poetry. Deceit, abstraction, euphemism: any one of these will doom a poem to the realm of "baffling" or "forgettable," or worse. Good poetry requires precision: if you do not attempt to say, accurately, truthfully, what you feel or see or need, then how will you achieve precision? What criterion will guide you to the next absolutely "right" word?*

—June Jordan (Muller 1995, 3)

The assignments in this book are split between writing and performance, with the early weeks of the workshop privileging writing because the most effective way of teaching spoken-word poetry uses the written word as the basis for performance. There is a reason for this initial emphasis on writing rather than performance: If a single written work can suggest many different modes of performance, each with a potentially different effect on the audience, then the entrance to those many effective pathways would remain shut without the solid foundation of a body of written work. If we didn't work hard in the first weeks of the workshop to generate effective writing, we would deprive both our naturally gifted writers and our student performers and at the same time.

In the fifth week of a Youth Speaks workshop, writing and performance converge. Students need two things at this point: to polish their writing through a series of intense revision exercises, and to become effective at performing their work. With only one week remaining before the culminating slam and with much of the workshop's writing already done, we are ready to begin this work. Knowing that a schoolwide performance awaits them at the end of the workshop gives students the resolve they need to begin a truly rigorous week of chiseling and polishing.

## The Final Week and the Process of Revision

Early in a workshop, we are especially careful not to privilege our academically better students by rewarding writing simply because it *looks* like the kind of poetry we're accustomed to reading. We want students who are prone to expressing themselves verbally, rather than through academic writing, to be as comfortable creating in the workshop as their more academically oriented peers are. We want students of all artistic and social backgrounds to be equally comfortable. To achieve that goal, we require that each written assignment be read aloud. This lets more verbally oriented poets read their words with the knowledge that how they sound and what they address takes precedence over how they are spelled or whether they violate grammatical or poetic rules. The workshop members can participate in dense criticism without having the nagging feeling that only the "best" students in the class are being rewarded—even more important, without having the feeling that their poetry is being judged on the basis of what is "educated" or "uneducated" about it, rather than on the fundamental stuff of spoken-word poetry itself: the heart of the matter, the issue confronted by a given poem, the dynamic rhythmic shifts in a poem's performance, to name just a few.

In the fifth and final week, when we have workshopped and performed poems for a month, students are ready to begin reading each other's work at an altogether more engaged level and to revise deeply. For this to happen, we must now have full access to the poem on the page. The month we have spent together has given the workshop members enough time to get familiar with each other as unique people with varied interests and experiences. The steady deepening of issues and exercises throughout the course has drawn the class to the point where the students can entrust each other with the awesome responsibility of readying each other for a performance in front of the entire school.

What does effective revision look like? The ways and methods of revision are too numerous to name. But at a fundamental level, revision always balances two things: the beauty a certain piece of writing already has, and its potential for achieving something even more effective. The goal is for young writers to improve their work without abandoning the power that the poems originally held. If a poem becomes clearer, shorter, or less complicated as a result of revision but loses what made it interesting or jolting, the revision isn't worth the time required to make it happen. If all we were aiming at as teachers was clarity or simplicity, we would be engaged in a different project than teaching poetry. In Youth Speaks workshops, we want more than anything to push our poets' writing and thinking further, whether a poem turns out to be thirty lines long, or fifty.

In the second week of a workshop, class members push themselves and their peer reviewers to develop every single important aspect of a poem to its logical limit. In this final week, we want to improve details, enhance rhythms, and find spots that could be expanded or chopped back to make the work flow more effectively. As we go through the revision process, we want the group to talk about which details are most effective and which can be improved. At these moments, the author is to remain silent so the audience will be as honest as possible about the work, without any guidance from the author herself.

As we push the poems as far as they can go, we make sure that the group is careful to express the positive aspects of each piece as well as what needs to be changed. Anyone who works with writers knows that nothing sinks deeper than a negative comment or the insistence that something needs to be changed in order for the piece to be effective. More than anything at this point, we are trying to engender students' confidence before the slam. This is a difficult time—a time when students feel vulnerable because their first real attempts at a polished work are brought before the class. To ease their tension, we begin the discussion of each poem with its positive aspects, and we use language from the lexicon of opportunity. Instead of feeling like they are visiting the firing line as the first victims of the editorial police, we want our writers to feel that this week gives them the opportunity to gain the confidence they'll need to perform at the slam for peers who have not been involved in the workshop. If student writers know what the workshop's members—including its teacher—really think about their poems, they will have a sense of how the school as a whole will receive them. In fact, given how much the students in the class work on refining, it is likely that others in the school will enjoy the poems even more than their authors do. Knowing this can do much to alleviate the tension that threatens to paralyze all speakers before a performance that makes them feel vulnerable.

In this fifth week of the workshop, students look for moments in each other's poems that need to be written more effectively for performance—moments that might jar the audience and break its concentration on and enjoyment of the poem. After they have identified such moments, we follow up by asking: Is this jarring a good thing—does it enhance the audience's experience of the poem? If the students decide it doesn't, they must find positive ways to criticize the poem and make it possible for the writer to change it, either by writing over the poem, or, in absolutely the last instance, by cutting it.

Because suggesting that a piece of writing be cut generally implies a "quick fix-it" method of "correcting" it rather than a commitment to develop the text more fully, we encourage our young poets to write *through* problematic moments in their pieces. We don't want them to be burdened by the thought that a jarring detail or unclear passage is a bad thing that needs to be excised in order for their poems to work smoothly. Instead, we want them to use initially problematic moments as opportunities to channel the energy in a passage—no matter how unclear or jolting it is—in a more effective direction. Cutting often feels like the way to make a poem better, if only because it eliminates the "problem" recognized by the students in the workshop. However, cutting usually ends up hurting the young writer because it robs her of the practice she'll need to be able to tackle difficult scenes, rhythms, and details later in her writing career. Especially if we consider writing poetry to be a lifetime's work, we must encourage fundamentals that will continue to reward our poets long after they leave our workshops.

Our method of revising is less like the work of an editor than that of a very interested friend who is excited about what a piece suggests to the imaginative mind. Taking this approach tends to mitigate the urge to clean up language and grammar, ferret out complicated passages, and so on—urges that are often more about limiting thought into some recognizable format than about expanding the work and making it resound more successfully with listeners' experience.

Student poets should critique each other's work with the *philosophy of coherence* beneath their comments. That's a heady-sounding phrase, but the workshop has been employing the philosophy all along. *Revising for coherence* means making suggestions for revising a poem by trying first to figure out the poem's central preoccupations. These preoccupations can range from style and theme to rhythm and sound or story and message. Only after we figure them out should we begin to wonder about sections of the poem that don't seem to fit, and about how they might be reshaped to surprise the audience in a more satisfying way.

Using this method of revision lets us avoid the drag that writing workshops can suffer when they get bogged down in questions of what the author intended. By the fifth week, we have already redefined *meaning* in our poems and we can now focus on what they are about—in terms of what they suggest to the workshop members. The students become a sounding board for what they think the poem means, and the author takes a back seat, trying to figure out ways to make her poem mean what she wants it to mean.

This revision method is standard in collegiate creative-writing classrooms. But for some reason, many of us did not experience it in high school. Judging from what relief and joy many of us who are now teachers felt when we found this kind of writing workshop in college, we expect explosive results when we invigorate high schools with the same revision method.

Because it has much to say about the basic means a poet uses to express her poem, the method of revising for coherence can also be extended to matters of meaning and style. To use the method in these areas, concentrate on the way a poem shifts between grammatical types and consider whether or not those types work together to form a cohesive poem. If the poetic grammar shifts over the course of a poem, it should shift for a reason. For instance, if a student is imitating a teacher's voice, that voice would use the grammar of the teacher. But as soon as the perspective shifted to a teenager's judgment of the teacher, the grammar would be relaxed (or, for a different effect, not) to lend a more effective mood to the piece. Students' and teachers' comments on revision should be directed toward effectivity rather than toward the notion that correct grammar should be spoken in all situations. English is as complicated as the diverse people who speak it, in all its dialects, accents, and tones, and if it is used to tell truths in new ways, it is not our duty to make that newness sound "proper"—it is our job to make those truths rise from the page to the sharpest possible effect.

## Revision Exercises for the Final Week

If a Youth Speaks workshop meets three times a week, on Monday of the fifth week we partner our poets in groups of two to four. We have asked them to bring in three printed copies of their poems, and today the workshop begins with the small groups reading all of its members' poems in turn, without pausing, writing, or saying anything.

After this first reading, each poet reads her work aloud to the small group, again, but this time the others read along and jot down moments in the piece that they admire or think could be better taken advantage of. After the poet has finished reading aloud, the group members read the poem to themselves in silence, using a simple revision key—underlining what they enjoy and using a squiggle to mark a place that is confusing or weak in comparison to the whole. Then each student writes three things on the back of the page:

1. What issues the poem seems to be concerned with, and what this draft of the poem means to this reader.
2. Two or three sentences of positive feedback about the details, timing, or topic of the piece.
3. At least three things that can be improved to give the poem greater effect, given the preoccupations and concerns of the poem as it is right now.

Directing the group to comment on work in this regimented way is effective for several reasons. For one, making the "poetic guess" of what the poem is really about ensures that readers are working to understand the piece and whether the poet has succeeded in conveying what she wanted to convey. If the rest of the feedback is mildly negative, the poet can use this first description to determine whether a reader understood what the poem was trying to achieve in the first place. The positive feedback will do much to explain what the reader enjoys and what could be changed for greater effect. Finally, this exercise helps every writer in the class get used to the idea that critical feedback on their work is required, which helps assuage the hurt feelings that can come from work that makes the writer feel especially vulnerable.

For homework Monday, students revise their poems in response to the peer comments. The teams of partners are given the task of improving each other's work, with the extra assignment of meeting on Tuesday for an intensive practice session.

On Wednesday, students read both their revised poems and the original to the entire workshop. Each student's partners from the small group tell the class what about the poem has changed. The workshop members then express what they like better about the revised piece, and what they like less. The teacher directs the group to think about the following questions:

1. Should the author put anything back in?
2. What works better in the revision than it did in the first draft?
3. What could still be added to enhance the piece?

Throughout Wednesday's workshop, we aim to keep comments as positive and useful as possible. Only a week remains before the slam performance, and the last thing we want to do with so little time left is to rattle the confidence of our poets or otherwise shut down the process of polishing their work. At the end of the day Wednesday, the teacher asks to keep the revised versions of all the poems and assigns students to do the same homework as on Monday, in the same order.

Between Wednesday and Friday, the teacher reviews the revised poems and writes feedback on them. On Friday, give the class a few minutes to read the feedback, then have a five-minute conference with each student to explain the comments. The teacher's job at this stage is to give confidence to the poet. Never underestimate the power of expressing how much the student has improved in the course, what strides she has made, and how much you look forward to hearing her work read aloud at the slam.

For the rest of the day on Friday, open the floor for a discussion of the one thing each student has brought to the workshop—a favorite poem (even one they have written), a piece of music, a talismanic object, and so on. Use this last class to enjoy each other's company in the knowledge that the group has worked very hard to come to know each other as individuals. After five weeks of learning to share each other's poetry, a workshop group has earned the right to share each other's company as whole and complex people at a deep, genuine, and heartfelt level. We conclude Youth Speaks workshops with a pep talk about what it means to have heard so many bright minds express themselves, and why this upcoming slam performance is only the beginning of a lifetime of such work.

## One Poet's Work

Adam Ng is one of the most gifted poets we have worked with, and is a member of the Youth Speaks advanced workshop and a recipient of the Tracie Morris Creative Writing and Spoken Word Award. Adam's use of detail, deep revision, and story make him one of the most arresting writers we have ever taught. When Adam first came to the workshops, it seemed he wanted to crawl out of his skin. Uncomfortable speaking in class, often quiet and reclusive, he might easily have slipped past our mentors' attention. Instead, the nurturing teaching style of Vanessa Wruble and Maria Archuleta brought Adam out of his shell. As a result of their good teaching, Youth Speaks gained a writer of untold potential. Here are Adam's student profile and his poems "From Out My Kitchen Window" and "During the Summer." As you read them, remember that Adam was just eighteen when he wrote them.

**Student Profile: Adam Ng**

My name is Adam Ng. I'm 18 years old and for four years I was a student at Brooklyn Tech. I've lived in Chinatown most of my life. Chinatown. The red place, with hallways and doors thickened with ageless layers of dust and paint red as blood, hardship and love red as petals of blood, the redolent ever-changing shiftless cradle of my childhood, a slum of sadness populated by overworked people's with whose febrile hopes lay enduring only in the promise of their growing children. When I am lost in Manhattan I look instinctively to the tops of buildings, trying to find evidence of it: Strained existence, its assorted vapors, the smells of its fishmarkets, the lucid sight of a butcher chopping a duck systematically into smaller and smaller portions . . . And all at the same time wishing it were a better, more contented place, for it to evolve beautifully within a short relieving sigh.

My mom works on the 4th floor in a sweatshop far down on Grand Street. For now, my father works at the Magic Wok restaurant in New Jersey. He used to get fired a lot when I was younger because he didn't take no lip from his bosses. Magic Wok something or other. Too faraway; he comes home only on Tuesdays.

Youth Speaks was introduced to me by two smiling graduate students, Vanessa Wruble and Maria Archuleta. They had come into the dreary, depressing air of a Brooklyn Tech classroom to teach a free workshop on fiction and short story writing. It seemed a strange situation i had entered into entirely by accident, with these stranger-girls who looked only a little older than i was, (from whom i would learn immensely), asking me who i was. I tended to distrust overt friendliness, so I probably wasn't very nice to them. Later that afternoon Vanessa, called my house (All the students of the workshop had shared phone-numbers). In school, I never cared about my grades. I had low grades mostly, around 75. There was this sense that I could trust what Youth Speaks was about. The last time a teacher or any faculty from school called it was from the school dean back in junior high school. I had gotten into a fight with a bully. The call was to inform my mother that I was suspended for two weeks.

Youth Speaks gave us the freedom to explore, to understand yourself and your interests is vital in realizing the things you most want to address through writing. For me, revision is about searching through the corners of your brain for that precise word, juggling the bits of a phrase like colorful lego for a tighter fit of sentence. I begin revision by mumbling through previous sections, making small marks, brackets, or question marks to note phrases or words that needed to be looked at, anything that seems awkward or digressing from the flow of poem. Then these parts (potholes) are revisited individually, starting from those easier to fix, and from there, working on each, letting the problem under a microscopic eye. This is the biggest part, the delirious mental action of shaping the line, twisting, and refitting the possible versions of phrasing until it becomes finally acceptable: increasingly accurate, essential, and fused with the rhythmic travel of syllables, the half-conscious meaning of what you're trying to say. By this time, the paper I write on becomes a trashed shred, a mess of gyred arrows, crossed out, double crossed wordings, and scratch looking letters.

I did only one revision for both "during the summer" and "from out my kitchen window." I remember the kitchen poem had a more improvised revision—I was still writing it, fudging the lines in my head before the performance. I had to go back and write out most of the poem afterwards.

I revise because it seems depressing for me to expend such care on writing something, fashioning the basic bones, then neglect the poem unfinished, denying its addition of flesh and final skin. I write most to extend a personal meaning to the reader or the audience, but that is something mostly imparted through the words. To not revise in most cases is to draw emotional generalities. I should probably edit and revise my work more. They never feel right until I do.

To perform a poem, I think, helps disperse doubt for both the poet and the audience. For the poet, it consoles that innate reservation always present in the periphery of the brain, that his/her words, merely dedicated to paper are fundamentally lifeless, unreaching like the book in the library no one has borrowed in five years. With the performance, there is a closeness as the culmination of evocative words permeates the air, and you as an individual of the audience is assured not by some abstract force alien to your heart, but by your own warm breath, blithe eye, and freedom of desire.

I think it is better concerning all things to be a child with wisdom than live as an adult who acts like a child. For a while in senior year at Tech I tossed the phrase Coolie Power around a lot but my friends didn't understand or seem to the love the idealism of the phrase as i did. Most of us, we are modern coolies—or will soon likely be stepping noiselessly into the shoes of one.

Youth Speaks introduced me to the poetry and the vibrancy of thought, clarity of consciousness, and

concern for the world around them, ardent voices acting as witness against the ongoing social injustices of
our time. It has made me realize how much I have not
done or said or written about in the same vein of brave
dissent. It's really up to me, the charged statement of
our society, with the design of words and dreams I will
take to create.

## From Out My Kitchen Window

**Adam Ng**

From out my kitchen window flow the murmurs of my
    house,
from within, redraws the thirst of my dying breath,
from thin, upon the kitchen table,
stirs the green plastic clock I bought on Canal Street,
the hungry electric rumble of a late-model Sanyo
    refrigerator,
the dry scratching of nails against dead skin.

From out my kitchen window,
against the grating,
I dream with the undercurrents of my soul,
of spring sheets tossed in summer's wind,
of jumping up into an endless sky,
and touching a dragonfly in passing.

## During the Summer

**Adam Ng**

During the summer I work at my father's hardware store,
selling hand-trucks and wrenches to balding middle-
    aged men with
protruding bellies,
wearing yellow sweat-stained t-shirts,

and tired depraved expressions.

(they stink like cigarettes, like a pack-a-day habit of
    Parliaments, or
Marlboros, or whatever it is they've been trying to kill
    themselves with.)

These guys that come in the hardware store, somehow,
they all look like my father,
or as if they could be somebody else's father,
as they talk down straight to my face,
for giving them the wrong kind of L-bracket,
or primer instead of finishing paint.
They talk to me the way all adults like to do,
when teenagers fuck up.

One day this old lady comes in the store looking to buy
a nice little push-cart for her Sunday grocery shopping.
She haggles me for half an hour over this stupid thing,
saying excitedly "Come on boy, $15.50, just five dollars
    less,
$15.50, $15.50."
and I keep telling her, "No ma'am I can't, I really can't,
    you see,
I can't."
But in the end I finally gave in and sold it to her for five
    dollars less,
even though my father always gives me this big shit
    about not giving in,
I did anyway,
because I knew how much five dollars was out of her
    social security check,
how many cats she could feed with five dollars,
And because, by then,
I was just too tired to resist.

When my father asked me how much I got for the cart I
    told him the truth.

He blew a gut;
he fired me.
I didn't blame him though.
I mean, if I were my father, owner of Ludlow Street
    Hardware,
I would have done the same.
I didn't care anyhow.

During the summer I think of a girl,
who stands and waits alone at DeKalb Station,
who takes the R but not the N,
who taps her foot secretly to some distant music,
as no one notices her but me.
And trying in vain to visualize the sad beauty of her face,
I pace in circles at the station,
imagining the places she might have walked,
and where the subway doors opened,
and where the subway doors would always close.

That night at the dinner table, over my mother's
    rendition of mashed potatoes and meat loaf,
I apologized to my father and asked for my job back,
trying not to let it show,
as I felt a little something inside me jerk and die away.
It was then that I finally understood my father,
and what he meant last fourth of July,
when he told me, drunk and cursing,
how a man is forced to forget his dreams and join the
    vast human fraternity
of the living-dead;
that to save a life one must also live to the bitter end.

What my father meant when he said it,
in a drunken despairing voice, was how sad it is,
to sell your sexy cow
to plough the blues.

## Four More Exercises for the Final Week: Performance and Revision

**1. Find the Hole in the Dream.** Great writing has often been likened to a dream that lets us suspend disbelief and enjoy the ride offered to us by the poet. This exercise is to identify moments in our pieces when that dream is broken. Have students bring three copies of their work to class. With the young poets working in groups of four, have each group read one poet's work and use a highlighter to mark passages in the poem where the dream is broken—that is, where audience members may momentarily lose interest. Then have the author perform the poem for the small group, giving the other students the choice of highlighting different passages based on what they hear or leaving their highlights the same. Each group should discuss how the poem and its performance can be improved, then repeat the process until each student has presented a poem to the small group.

**2. The Vision of Revision.** Writers often need an unexpected insight to revise effectively, something that breaks the shape of how we originally conceived our writing. For this exercise, ask your students to bring in a poem they have reworked extensively, then ask them to rewrite either the entire poem or its essential core as a single mathematical equation. Tell them that this revised version of the same poem will look and feel different from the poem itself—its job is to help us break down barriers to revision. Don't worry if your students look confused when you ask them to do this—simply see what they can do. After they've created their equations, have them write the poem again, but this time working from the equation, not the original text. The poems will change greatly in this second exercise. Have all the students read their work to the whole group, each time having the students discuss whether they like the first poem or the last one better, and why.

*3. A Font by Any Other Name.* This exercise has students consider the way font styles—and, by extension, speaking styles—can affect the meaning of the poems we write. Ask students to bring in one poem that is printed four times, in four fonts of radically different sizes and moods. Have the class look at each poem and pick the font they like best given the poem's subject matter and flow. Set this version aside and have them pick the font they like least for the poem. Discuss how the tone and mood of the font suggests different ways for the poem to be effectively rewritten, then add to, revise, and cut the poem until it feels more satisfying. Show the original writer the "best" version and the revised version side-by-side. (In a related exercise, have students read the poems out loud using different voices and tones to represent different fonts according to the way the words look on the page.) Ask your students to revise their poems after class using what they took from the discussion.

*4. Revision's Excess.* Have students pass their poems to the left. Each student reads in silence or silently a two-line section of the poem she has and adds a word, phrase, or sentence. The addition should be something that makes the section more specific or effective. This first step should take no longer than thirty seconds. After it is finished, have everyone pass the poems to the left again and repeat the process until each poem has at least fifteen additions. Then have the poet look at her original work, consider the suggested changes, and rewrite the poem on a separate piece of paper, incorporating the additions she likes. Ask several of your writers to perform their revised pieces.

# ■ ■ ■ ■ Letting the Poets Speak: The Poetry Event

*With Youth Speaks' help, my writing and performance abilities have strengthened, and so has my self-confidence. Now I am a confident performer and I am able to share my words with an audience, without the ordeal of shaky legs and a palpitating heart. After walking off the stage for the first time I knew that I would be back again and again and again. The rush that I feel from a performance is what skydivers look for or think they have found.*

—Eliza K. Shrader, 17

*I am not a coward anymore*
*I see us for what we are*
*nothing less than great, because*
*we are the poets . . .*

*we walk and talk mountains*
*breathe hurricanes, hum earthquakes*
*and our kisses are wet haikus glistening on crimson pages*

—Tim Arevalo (Sonnie 2000, 125)

When you begin to notice that the shyest students raise their hand to read their poems in class or that the pages of their writing notebooks are tattered and filling up with words, it's time to celebrate! A spoken-word poetry event is a special, extraordinary school event, both a celebration and a means for growth and development. These events are the highpoint of the Youth Speaks model of teaching. The classroom is left behind and the hard work of writing is replaced by the thrill the poet gets from performing before his peers *in his own language*. No experience is more nerve-racking, adrenaline pumping, or rewarding than the first time a young poet performs his work before peers.

A spoken-word poetry event has both educational usefulness and profound personal advantages for students. When teen poets are introduced to each other and to the outside world, poetry becomes a home for experimentation and self-exposure. Teenagers have so few places where they can congregate and be "real" with each other. These poetry events, if they're successful, become occasions for the most enlightened kind of youth community to occur. Adults and young people alike need to hear poetry to appreciate it. As young writers learn to love the sounds of their own voices, it becomes much easier for them to love the sounds of other voices— other poets, other teachers, other people. After their initial fear subsides, teen poets clamor to get to a mic and they begin to write more often and for others. Teen poetry events, together with consistent exposure to a workshop environment, offer teenagers a medium for a new kind of creative, self-revelatory expression.

## Slam or Open Mic?

A *poetry slam* is a competition in which poets are given scores based on both performance and writing. As your workshop nears its end, decide what kind of event your students are ready for. If they are needy or hesitant with their writing and don't seem confident enough to compete, it's safer—and usually as much fun—to run an open mic. If your school is small and your students exceedingly confident, try a slam, a fun, nonstressful competition for bragging rights.

If your workshop students have had a chance to work on memorization, an open mic will let them try their hand at it. If they forget some lines here and there, no worries: They can either refer to a copy of the poem kept in their pocket or try freestyling— improvising the poem—on the spot. This experiment will only enhance their skills and ready them for future performances.

With either a slam or an open mic event, you will need to find an emcee to host and a deejay. The emcee for an open mic needs to be someone—not a teacher, perhaps a student—who can be sensitive and encouraging to everyone who steps up to the mic. At Youth Speaks we have begun to let the teen poets themselves emcee the open mic events. Enabling young people to do and speak for themselves is a key way for them to feed the community of poets they come from.

A *deejay* is needed to create ambiance. Youth culture is dependent on music for ambiance, energy, juice, and celebration. If there's a student deejay available, ask him ahead of time to provide music for the event. Make sure there's an outlet for a sound system or a stereo boombox. Music should already be playing at the beginning of the event, when students are taking their seats, and should play in the time it takes for each poet to get up on stage after the emcee announces the name. Of course, when a poet is performing, the room should be silent; the audience respectful. It is the job of the emcee to ensure this.

If you've decided to do a slam, you will need three or five impartial judges and a scorekeeper. At least for your first slams, the judges should not be students. Each judge rates a poem on a scale of 1 to 10, with a maximum of 5 for performance and 5 for writing, using his or her own aesthetics preferences for performed poetry. Depending on whether you decide to have the emcee read the scores aloud after each performer or kept to the very end, judges write their scores on a sheet of paper and the scorekeeper records them and calculates the average (minus high and low scores if there are five judges). If you decide to announce the scores, the emcee should go from low to high when reading them out after a poet reaches his seat. Get the average score quickly from the scorekeeper and excitedly shout it out. Judges should not take their jobs too seriously, and no scores should be lower than 6. The key to a slam is to encourage poets by applauding the poetry, not the scores.

## Thinking Things Through

Though it will require some planning, putting on a spoken-word poetry event will be rewarding enough to warrant all the work. Enlist the help of other teachers and administrators to generate excitement about the event throughout school. As the event draws near, put up posters or circulate flyers around school. The event itself should come as no surprise to your students, so determine the date and type of event at least two weeks before. Make it mandatory for every one of your workshop students to perform and have them pick the poem they'll perform ahead of time. The poem should be one they're comfortable with, that they've read aloud in class and revised at least once. If you can, spend some workshop time working on memorization techniques.

No matter how well-prepared they are, the students will be nervous. Put their nervous energy to work. This event is for them, so let them be involved in creating it. To ensure a lively event, consider what your time and resources permit, then go about getting as many people involved as possible. The more involved the students are, the more they will look forward to the event. Try to create a warm environment. If you must use the school cafeteria, for example, check to see where the stage and microphone will be set up, how chairs should be arranged, where the deejay can plug in, whether the lights can be dimmed, and whether the sound will carry. Coordinate a fast-paced, entertaining show. Are there student deejays who can provide music before and between the poems? Is there a teen artist who can create a banner or mural to hang behind the stage?

## Emceeing the Event

Finding a good emcee isn't easy. The emcee's basic responsibilities include calling up the poets, keeping the event moving, and, most important, generating love and applause from the crowd for each poet. A good emcee can fill in blank spaces, reduce competitive juices, keep the audience excited and positive, raise the level of cheering for a vulnerable poem, ask for more clapping from the audience after a poem, and dole out compliments evenly to all poets, good or great. Try to find a young adult poet in the community who will "give it up" to the student poets and respect their electricity and authenticity. If you can't find a poet, consider using a student emcee who can manage the job and be good to all the poets—it's best to use a young emcee for this youth event. If those resources fail, ask a friendly school administrator to emcee—or do it yourself.

## The Teacher's Role

As coordinator of the event, your mind will be on the details. Hopefully most of them will have been completed ahead of time. Be prepared to give a short introduction to the event, reminding the audience to be respectful to the poets and introducing the emcee. Be present enough to enjoy and congratulate each of your students, and to soak up some of the striking moments in their performances. After all your hard work, it is time to see your students in a new light. Sit back, enjoy, and revel in the poetry you hear. This is only the beginning of what your students will accomplish.

## Checklist for Your Spoken-Word Poetry Event

1. Decide what kind of event it will be: slam or open mic.
2. Set the date, time, and place with plenty of lead time. Each poet will have no more than three minutes. Decide how long the event will be based on the number of poets. An hour is sufficient for most full-size classes (thirty students).
3. Make the performance mandatory for all your workshop students.
4. Involve your students in planning and promoting the event.

5. Let the students create the event materials and pass them out. Create an image for a flyer or poster. Make sure the materials include all pertinent information.

6. Determine whether you need a microphone, a stage, or other audio-visual equipment.

7. Find your emcee and make sure he knows the routine ahead of time.

8. Transform the space. How's the seating? Are there enough chairs? Are the lights too bright? Is the space quiet enough for poetry? Is there time to create a mural to hang behind the stage?

9. Start an attendance list. Decide whether students can invite parents and friends from other classes. If so, how many guests can each poet invite? (Parents are not often on the top of the list.) Decide whether to allow students from other classes to perform too.

10. Create ambiance. Is there a student deejay who can play music before and between poems, or can you pay a local deejay to spin? Do you have specific music requirements?

11. Decide how the poets will be called up to the mic—in a particular order? In random order? With the emcee drawing names out of a hat? Should one poet be "on deck" to prevent lag time?

12. Make students aware of any rules they must follow. Is their language choice limited? Can they use a beat box under their poem? Can they perform in groups?

13. Get three or five judges and a scorekeeper and make sure they have all the supplies they need: sheets of paper, black markers, pads to scribble on, a calculator, water.

14. Decide if the scores are going to be read out loud after every poet, or if the winner will be announced at the end.

15. Get ready to deliver an introduction to remind the audience that they're there to enjoy the poetry and the poets and to show as much love as possible.

16. Decide who will introduce the event to the audience. This person will explain how a slam or open mic works, what the rules are, and how the audience should act, reminding the audience that the event is first and foremost an expression of creative minds at work and they are here to enjoy the voices and give their support, expressing as much love for the poets as possible.

17. Do any clean-up that's necessary.

18. Remember to follow up in class provided you continue on in regular English class.

# Glossary

*alliteration.* A poetic device of repeating and stacking words that use the same sound. The repetition can be of consonants (*consonance*) or vowels (*assonance*).

*assonance.* The repetition of vowel sounds; a form of *alliteration.*

*consonance.* The repetition of consonant sounds; a form of *alliteration.*

*detail-hunting.* A method of studying a poem by focusing on its specific details, rather than on the overall effect of its message.

*deejay (also DJ).* The person who adds atmosphere to a spoken-word poetry event by playing music between performances and providing rhythmic tracks for performers who want to read their poetry to an established beat.

*emcee (also MC).* The host of an event, who entertains the audience, comments positively on each performer's work, and introduces performers.

*freestyle.* A type of improvisational poetry that the poet develops onstage from a set of words or concepts (perhaps suggested by the audience). Rather than celebrating the compact expression of dense poetic *conceits* (images that control the development of a poem), freestyle poems develop from rhymes and repetition, embracing surprise, rhythmic consistency, and expansiveness.

*genius-producing exercises.* Exercises that are simultaneously low-risk and highly evocative, and are productive and powerful tools for voicing student creativity. Such exercises give the correct impression that students are overflowing with ideas for effective writing.

*hip-hop.* Hip-hop is a culture that embodies four elements of art and musical expression: emceeing, deejaying, graffiti, and breakdancing. Wendy Day defines it as "life seen through the eyes of an entire generation." For a helpful discussion of this culturally complex term, see *Black Noise* by Tricia Rose (1994) and Nelson George's *Hip-Hop America* (1998).

*internal rhyme.* A poetic device of using rhymes in places other than at the end of the line, whether within a single line or between lines, buried within the phrasing of the poem.

*onomatopoeia.* A device of using words and phrases that sound like what they mean (for example, *meow* and *sizzle*).

*open mic.* A noncompetitive spoken-word poetry event that is open to all performers.

*performance.* In the context of spoken-word poetry, relating aloud of a poem. A performance can range from simple narration to a full theatrical presentation.

*revising for clarity.* A technique of editing that seeks to render a text as clear as possible along one interpretive line. This method usually results in cutting a text back to achieve the intended effect. We advise against using this technique in spoken-word poetry workshops.

*revising for coherence.* A technique of refining writing by uncovering a text's preoccupations through close reading or by questioning the author, then making that preoccupation come to life in as many aspects of the text (and performance) as possible.

*significant tone.* Using one's voice to convey new and usually essential meaning to a word, phrase, or sentence in a poetic context. For a useful discussion of this technique in a musical context, see *Blues People* by LeRoi Jones (1963).

*slam. n.* A poetry competition in which poets perform their own work for an audience and are judged on the basis of both writing and performance. v. To perform poetry before an audience in a slam competition.

*spoken-word poetry.* Poetry that is written on a page but per-formed for an audience. Because it is performed, this poetry tends to forefront rhythm, improvisation, free association, rhymes, and the use of hybrid language, from rich poetic phras-ing to the gritty imagery of the vernacular.

*sprung rhythm.* A poetic device, invented by Gerard Manley Hopkins, for creating rhythmic flows within a single poetic line by densely packing alliterative phrases that, when read, sound markedly different from the rhythms and phrasings of everyday language, thus creating the feeling of a new internal rhythm within the lines of the poem itself.

*terza rima.* A poetic rhyme scheme of three-line stanzas that rhyme *aba, bcb, cdc*, etc. For a fine description of this form and many others, consult *The Teachers and Writers Handbook of Poetic Forms* (Padgett 1987).

# Works Cited

Brandon, Ruth. 1999. *Surreal Lives.* New York: Grove Press.

Gardner, Howard. 1993. *Multiple Intelligences: The Theory in Practice.* New York: Basic Books.

Gramsci, Antonio. 1971. *Selections from the Prison Notebooks.* New York: International Publishers.

Greene, Maxine. 1995. *Releasing the Imagination.* San Francisco: Jossey-Bass.

Jones, LeRoi (a.k.a. Amiri Baraka). 1968. *Black Music.* New York: DeCapo Press.

———. 1963. *Blues People: Negro Music in White America.* New York: Morrow Quill Paperbacks.

Jordan, June. 1993. *Haruko/Love Poems.* New York: Serpent's Tail.

Lorde, Audre. 1996. *Sister Outsider.* London: Pandora.

Mahiri, Jabari. 1998. *Shooting for Excellence.* New York: NCTE and Teachers College Press.

Morris, Tracie. 1998. *Intermission.* New York: Soft Skull Press.

Muller, Lauren, ed. 1995. *June Jordan's Poetry for the People.* New York: Routledge.

Padgett, Ron, ed. 1987. *The Teachers and Writers Handbook of Poetic Forms.* New York: Teachers and Writers Collaborative.

Powell, Kevin. 1999. "Notes from a Hip-Hop Head." *Hip-Hop: A Cultural Expression.* CSU Conference.

Rich, Adrienne. 1993. *What Is Found There.* New York: Norton.

Rukeyser, Muriel. 1996. *The Life of Poetry.* Ashfield, MA: Paris Press.

Sonnie, Amy, ed. 2000. *Revolutionary Voices.* Los Angeles: Alyson Books.

Weiss, Jennifer, ed. 2000. *Speak Your Mind, Volume 2: The Youth Speaks Anthology of Spoken Word Poetry.* New York: Youth Speaks Press.

## Selected Works on Spoken-Word Poetry and Hip-Hop

Algarin, Miguel and Bob Holman, eds. 1994. *Aloud: Voices from the Nuyorican Poets Café.* New York: Owl Books.

Anglessey, Zoe, ed. 1999. *Listen Up! Spoken Word Poetry.* New York: The Ballantine Publishing Group.

Dent, Gina, ed. 1998. *Black Popular Culture: A Project by Michele Wallace.* New York: The New Press. (First pub. 1983 by Bay Press.)

George, Nelson. 1998. *Hip-Hop America.* New York: Viking.

Rose, Tricia. 1994. *Black Noise.* Hanover, MA: Wesleyan University Press.